Excel 2002

Level 1

Allison K. P. Clark

Jeannine P. Pray

Excel 2002: Level 1

Part Number: 084200
Course Edition: 3.0

ACKNOWLEDGMENTS

Project Team

Curriculum Developer and Technical Writer: Allison K. P. Clark • **Sr. Curriculum Developer and Technical Writer:** Jeannine P. Pray • **Copy Editors:** Christy D. Johnson and Taryn Chase • **Technical Editor:** Dominique Fantuzzo • **Print Designer:** Daniel Smith • **Content Manager:** Cheryl Russo

NOTICES

HELP US IMPROVE OUR COURSEWARE

Your comments are important to us. Please contact us at Element K Press LLC, 1-800-478-7788, 500 Canal View Boulevard, Rochester, NY 14623, Attention: Product Planning, or through our Web site at **http://support.elementkcourseware.com.**

**Approved
Courseware**

This logo means that this courseware has been approved by the Microsoft® Office Specialist Program to be among the finest available for learning Microsoft Excel 2002. It also means that upon completion of this courseware, you may be prepared to take an exam for Microsoft Office Specialist qualification.

What is a Microsoft Office Specialist? A Microsoft Office Specialist is an individual who has passed exams for certifying his or her skills in one or more of the Microsoft Office desktop applications such as Microsoft Word, Microsoft Excel, Microsoft PowerPoint, Microsoft Outlook, Microsoft Access, or Microsoft Project. The Microsoft Office Specialist Program typically offers certification exams at the "Core" and "Expert" skill levels. The Microsoft Office Specialist Program is the only program in the world approved by Microsoft for testing proficiency in Microsoft Office desktop applications and Microsoft Project. This testing program can be a valuable asset in any job search or career advancement.

To learn more about becoming a Microsoft Office Specialist, visit **www.microsoft.com/officespecialist**. To learn more about other Microsoft Office Specialist approved courseware from Element K, visit **www.elementkcourseware.com**.

*The availability of Microsoft Office Specialist certification exams varies by application, application version, and language. Visit **www.microsoft.com/officespecialist** for exam availability.

Microsoft, the Microsoft Office Logo, PowerPoint, and Outlook are trademarks or registered trademarks of Microsoft Corporation in the United States and/or other countries, and the Microsoft Office Specialist Logo is used under license from owner.

Element K is independent from Microsoft Corporation, and not affiliated with Microsoft in any manner. This publication may be used in assisting students to prepare for a Microsoft Office Specialist Exam. Neither Microsoft, its designated program administrator or courseware reviewer, nor Element K warrants that use of this publication will ensure passing the relevant exam.

NOTES

EXCEL 2002: LEVEL 1

CONTENTS

CONTENTS

APPENDIX A: COMMON PROBLEMS ASSOCIATED WITH PRINTING

APPENDIX B: MICROSOFT OFFICE SPECIALIST PROGRAM

APPENDIX C: INTERNET AND COMPUTING CORE CERTIFICATION (IC^3)
PROGRAM

ABOUT THIS COURSE

This course, *Excel 2002: Level 1,* is the first course in a series. This course will give you the skills to create, edit, format, and print basic worksheets and charts in Excel.

As you probably know, working with numeric data on a regular basis can be a very tedious process, especially if you have tables containing many rows and columns of data listed on paper. The simplest change can result in lost time erasing, rewriting, and fixing incorrect computations. By using Excel to create an electronic version (called worksheets) of your paper data, much of your work becomes automated, making it easier to manage numbers and calculations. The simplest change is no longer a burden. In addition, your worksheets will look neat and will be formatted, making the data easy to read and interpret.

Course Description

Target Student

Persons desiring to prepare to be a certified Microsoft Office User Specialist (MOUS) in Excel, and who already have knowledge of Microsoft Windows 98 or above operating system, and desire to gain the skills necessary to create, edit, format, and print basic worksheets and charts in Excel.

Course Prerequisites

To ensure your success, we recommend you first take the following Element K course or have equivalent knowledge:

* *Windows 2000: Introduction*

How To Use This Book

As a Learning Guide

Each lesson covers one broad topic or set of related topics. Lessons are arranged in order of increasing proficiency with *Microsoft Excel*; skills you acquire in one lesson are used and developed in subsequent lessons. For this reason you should work through the lessons in sequence.

We organized each lesson into results-oriented topics. Topics include all the relevant and supporting information you need to master *Microsoft Excel*, activities allow you to apply this information to practical hands-on examples.

You get to try out each new skill on a specially prepared sample file. This saves you typing time and allows you to concentrate on the skill at hand. Through the use of sample files, hands-on activities, illustrations that give you feedback at crucial steps, and supporting background information, this book provides you with the foundation and structure to learn *Microsoft Excel* quickly and easily.

As a Review Tool

Any method of instruction is only as effective as the time and effort you are willing to invest in it. In addition, some of the information that you learn in class may not be important to you immediately, but it may become important later on. For this reason, we encourage you to spend some time reviewing the topics and activities after the course. For additional challenge when reviewing activities, try the What You Do column before looking at the How You Do It column.

As a Reference

The organization and layout of the book makes it easy to use as a learning tool and as an after-class reference. You can use this book as a first source for definitions of terms, background information on given topics, and summaries of procedures.

Course Objectives:

In this course, you will create basic worksheets and charts.

You will:

- create a basic worksheet by entering text and values.
- work with cells and cell data by using a variety of moving and copying techniques.
- perform calculations on data by using formulas, including functions.
- change the appearance of worksheet data by using a variety of formatting techniques.
- work with multiple worksheets by formatting, repositioning, copying and moving, and adding and deleting worksheets within a workbook.
- create and modify charts.
- set the page display and printing options.

Course Requirements:

Hardware

- A Pentium 133 MHz or higher processor required for all operating systems.
- A minimum of 64 MB of RAM, recommended, for Windows 2000 Professional; in addition, you should have 8 MB of RAM for each application running simultaneously. (Note: Memory requirements may differ for other operating systems.)
- A minimum of 516 MB of free hard disk space. (Under Windows 2000, at least 4 MB of space must be available in the Registry.)
- Either a local CD-ROM drive or access to a networked CD-ROM drive.
- A floppy-disk drive.
- A two-button mouse, an IntelliMouse, or compatible pointing device.
- A VGA or higher-resolution monitor; Super VGA recommended.
- An installed printer driver.
- A sound card.

Software

- A custom installation of Microsoft Office XP Professional—see the Class Setup Requirements for additional instructions.

Class Setup

This book was written using the Windows 2000 Professional operating system. Using this book with other operating systems may affect how the activities work. Note: The manufacturer states that Microsoft Office XP Professional with FrontPage will work with Microsoft Windows 98, Microsoft Windows ME, and Microsoft Windows NT Workstation 4.0. Office XP Professional with FrontPage will not run on the Microsoft Windows 3.x, Microsoft Windows NT 3.5x, or Microsoft Windows 95 operating systems.

1. Install Windows 2000 Professional on a newly formatted hard drive.
2. If the Getting Started With Windows 2000 window is displayed, uncheck Show This Screen At Startup and click Exit.
3. Install a printer driver.

   A printer isn't necessary for class, but you must have a printer driver installed.

4. A complete installation of Microsoft Office XP Professional with FrontPage.

   Steps 1 through 4 need to be done only once. Steps 5 through 7 must be done before every class to ensure a proper setup.

5. On the students' computers, reset the usage data. (Choose Tools→Customize and click Reset My Usage Data to restore the default settings.)
6. Delete the folder C:\My Documents\Excel.

7.   Run the self-extracting data file located on the data disk. This will place the data in the My Documents folder. (Verify where you want the data files located.)

List of Additional Files

Printed with each activity is a list of files students open to complete that activity. Many activities also require additional files that students do not open, but are needed to support the file(s) students are working with. These supporting files are included with the student data files on the course CD-ROM or data disk. Do not delete these files.

LESSON 1
Getting Started

Lesson Objectives:

In this lesson, you will create a basic worksheet by entering text and values.

You will:

- Identify the uses of Excel.
- Open Excel and use the keyboard and mouse to enter data in a worksheet.
- Edit data in a worksheet by using a variety of editing techniques.
- Format data to change its appearance.
- Save a new file by using the Save As command.
- Use the Ask A Question box to access Help.

Introduction

At this point, you've probably worked with tables of data on paper—perhaps even a paper ledger like the one shown in Figure 1-1, but not with Microsoft Excel. In this lesson, you will create an electronic version of your paper data. Specifically, you will enter, replace, edit, and change data.

You have this great piece of software in your hands and a table of values entered in rows and columns on paper that you need to enter in Excel. An example of your paper data appears in Figure 1-1. However, you're not sure how to use the software. The first step is to enter the data. Then, you can edit and format the data. Before you know it, your data will be entered in an electronic format—staring back at you from Excel.

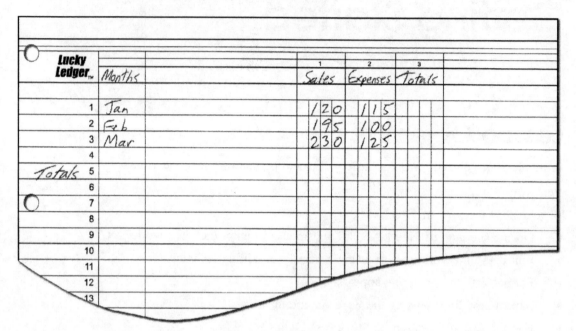

Figure 1-1: *An example of a paper spreadsheet.*

TOPIC A

Identify What You Can Do with Excel

Excel is installed on your PC, but you're not sure how you should use it in your job. In this topic, you will identify what you can do with Excel.

The Excel program is open. You're staring at the screen saying to yourself, "Now what do I do?" Knowing what you can do in Excel is the first step toward completing your first worksheet.

Identify What You Can Do with Excel

If you've ever used a paper spreadsheet, you know how cumbersome it can be. Making changes can be time consuming, and you increase the chance of making errors in calculations.

Definition

Excel is a software application that provides an electronic spreadsheet, or worksheet, environment you use to manage numbers and calculations. An Excel file, called a *workbook,* can contain several worksheets. The *worksheet* is where you enter text, numbers, and formulas. By default, each workbook contains three worksheets.

Example

Unlike a paper spreadsheet, you can set up an Excel workbook as a responsive and dynamic work environment. Excel offers a number of useful features that allow you to:

- Create formulas that are automatically updated when you change your data.
- Organize lists of data by sorting, filtering, and summarizing data.
- Plot numeric data in charts.
- Automate and customize procedures by using macros.

Non-Example

You would not use Excel to:

- Complete word processing tasks.
- Create a *database* of information.
- Create a slide presentation.

DISCOVERY ACTIVITY 1-1

Identifying Uses of Excel

Objective:

Identify examples where Excel is used correctly.

Scenario:

Your boss gives you a list of tasks to complete by the end of the week. You aren't sure if you should use Excel to complete each task or another software application. In this activity, you will decide in what situations it's best to use Excel to accomplish the task indicated.

1. **In the following table, indicate Yes if you would use Excel to accomplish the task or No if you would use another software application to accomplish the task.**

Task	Your Response
You need to create a chart that is linked to a range of data.	
You need to create a list of sales data that includes commission calculations and then sort and filter that data a number of ways.	
You need to create a memo to all department managers.	
You need to create a database of customers and their addresses.	
You need to compose a letter to one of your boss's associates.	
You need to create a monthly budget for your department.	

2. **Which task is best accomplished by using Excel?**

    a) Create a database of your company's client base.

    b) Calculate sales data for three divisions in your company.

    c) Create a table that includes employee service award intervals and their corresponding gifts.

    d) Create a presentation that includes a table with numerical data.

TOPIC B

Enter Data in a Worksheet

Now that you know what tasks you can accomplish with Excel, you'll want to get started. In this topic, you'll enter data in a worksheet.

Unless you enter some data in your worksheet, it won't be useful to you. A worksheet without data is like a bookshelf without books. However, once you enter data in a worksheet, then you can begin to manipulate it to suit your needs.

The Workbook Environment

Now you're ready to start Excel. When you do, two windows are displayed, one within the other. The outer window is the application window, and the inner window is the workbook window. The *application window* usually fills the entire screen and provides an interface for you to interact with Excel. The *workbook window* appears within the application window and displays a workbook in which to enter and store data.

The default Excel *workbook* contains three *worksheets* named Sheet1 through Sheet3. The sheet names appear on tabs at the bottom of the workbook. A new Excel workbook file can contain up to 255 separate worksheets.

Each worksheet is made up of cells. A *cell* is the intersection of a column and a row. When you open a new workbook, the cell that's selected is the *active cell.*

The Excel worksheet is a grid of 256 columns by 65,536 rows. A *column* is a boundary within a worksheet that extends vertically through all the rows and holds data. A *row* is a boundary within a worksheet that extends horizontally through all of the columns and holds data. By default, Excel designates columns by letters running across the top of the worksheet, and designates rows by numbers running down the left border of the worksheet. Column headings begin with the letter A and continue through the letter Z. After the 26th column (column Z), headings become double letters, from AA to IV. Row headings begin with the number 1 and continue through the number 65536. Figure 1-2 shows the location of each element in the Excel application environment.

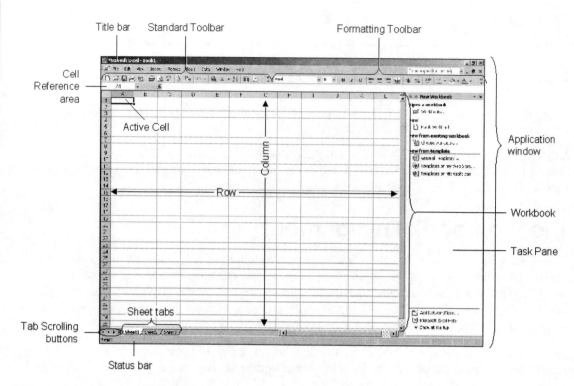

Figure 1-2: *The workbook environment.*

Table 1-1 defines the features of a workbook that you need to be familiar with when using Excel.

Table 1-1: *Excel Window Elements*

Window Element	Location	Definition
Application window	Usually fits entire screen	Larger of the two start-up windows; provides an interface for you to interact with the Excel application.
Title bar	Across the top of the application window	Displays the name of the application and the active workbook.
Toolbars	Below the menu bar—the Standard toolbar is on the left; the Formatting toolbar is on the right	The Standard toolbar provides quick access to Excel's most frequently used commands. The Formatting toolbar provides access to common formatting features.
Formula bar	Below the Formatting toolbar	Displays the contents of the active cell in a workbook.
Cell reference area	Above the column A heading	Displays the name of the current or active cell.
Active cell	By default, cell A1	The cell that's currently selected.
Cell	Within the workbook	Intersection of a column and a row.
Column	Within the workbook	A boundary within a worksheet that extends vertically through all of the rows and holds data.
Row	Within the workbook	A boundary within a worksheet that extends horizontally through all of the columns and holds data.

Window Element	Location	Definition
Status bar	Below the workbook	Displays information about a selected command and Excel's current state.
Workbook	Within the application window	Smaller of the two start-up windows; an area you can use to work and store data in.
Sheet tabs	At the bottom of the workbook	Allow you to move from one sheet to another in a workbook.
Tab scrolling buttons	To the left of the sheet tabs	Scroll the display of sheet tabs one at a time, or display the first or last grouping of sheet tabs within a workbook.

What is the Mode Indicator?

Definition

The *mode indicator* appears on the left side of the status bar and indicates the status of the active cell. When you're entering data, you might want to refer to the mode indicator. Its three modes are outlined in the following table.

Mode	Description
Ready	Displays when the active cell is selected.
Enter	Displays when you're entering data in the active cell.
Edit	Displays when you're editing data in the active cell.

Example

Suppose you have cell A3 selected. The mode indicator displays Ready. You begin typing in cell A3. The mode indicator changes to Enter. After you enter the data, you decide you need to change the data. You press [F2]. The mode indicator changes to Edit.

 Often, it may seem like Excel is not working. However, you may have just forgotten to press the [Enter] key.

Enter Data in a Worksheet

Procedure Reference: Enter Data in an Excel Worksheet

When you're ready to enter data in an Excel worksheet, the suggested order is:

1. Type the text information to create a structure.

2. Type the numerical information within the structure.

3. Add the formulas, copying where possible.

4. Add a title to the worksheet.

5. Format the text, numbers, and formulas.

Default Data Formatting

To create your own workbook in Excel, you'll need to enter data. Worksheet cells can contain constant values (text or numbers) or formulas. In a worksheet, you use text to organize and identify the numerical information. By default, text appears left-aligned in a cell and numbers appear right-aligned in a cell.

ACTIVITY 1-2

Entering Data

Setup:

The Windows 2000 desktop is displayed.

Scenario:

You just sat down at your desk to begin the day's work, and your boss hands you a handwritten paper spreadsheet that he wants you to enter in Excel by 2:00 P.M. this afternoon. A copy of that spreadsheet appears in Figure 1-3. In this activity, you will enter the data in a new worksheet.

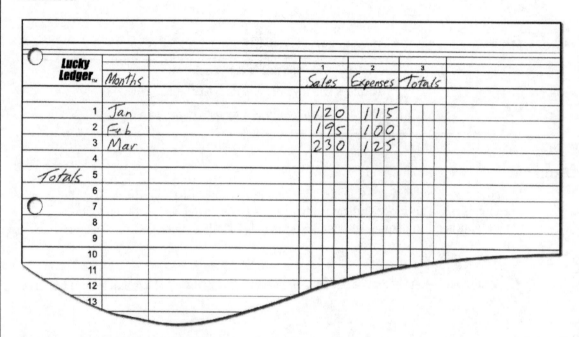

Figure 1-3: *A sample of your boss's paper spreadsheet.*

What You Do	How You Do It
1. Start Excel.	a. From the Windows taskbar, **click Start.**
	b. **Choose Programs→Microsoft Excel.**

2. In the following graphic, identify the columns, rows, and cells in the worksheet.

    Column ___

    Row ___

    Cell ___

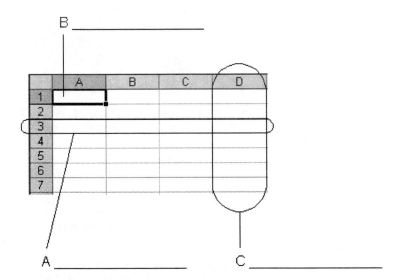

3. **Identify the active cell.**

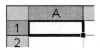

4. **Identify the text in the cell reference area.**

    A1 ▾ *fx*

5. **What is the status of the mode indicator?**

    |◄ ◄ ► ►|\Sheet1
    Ready

6. In cell A2, **type *Months*, but don't press [Enter].**

    a. **Place the mouse pointer on cell A2. It appears as a hollow cross.**

    b. **Click the mouse button** to select cell A2. Now, you're ready to enter some text.

    c. **Type *Months*, but don't press [Enter].** This is one of the headings for your worksheet. The word appears in both the Formula bar and in the cell, but you haven't entered it yet.

---

7. **Identify the buttons in the Formula bar and the status of the mode indicator.**

    a. On the Formula bar, **identify the Cancel, Enter, and Insert Function buttons.**

    You can use these buttons for data entry.

    b. **Identify the status of the mode indicator.** The mode is Enter because you're in the process of entering data.

📌 To enter data, you can also use the Enter button or select another cell. There are additional methods for entering data that will be discussed later.

8. **Finish entering the text.**

    a. **Press [Enter]** to enter the text and move down one cell. By default, text appears left-aligned in the cell. Cell A3 is now the active cell. Let's enter some more data.

---

9. In cell B2, **enter *Sales*.**

    a. **Select cell B2.** You can either click on the cell or use the [→] and [↑] keys to select cell B2.

b. Type *Sales* and press [Enter] to enter the text in cell B2. The active cell is now B3.

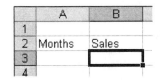

	A	B
1		
2	Months	Sales
3		
4		

Now, let's enter a number.

10. In cell B3, **enter 120 and look at the right-aligned entry.**

a. **Verify that cell B3 is selected.**

b. **Type 120 and press [Enter].**

c. **Look at the number in cell B3.** Excel displays the number as right-aligned.

Now, you can enter data on your own.

PRACTICE ACTIVITY 1-3

Completing the Worksheet

Activity Time:

15 minutes

Scenario:

Now that you know how to enter text and numbers in a worksheet, you're going to finish entering the data.

	A	B	C	D
1				
2	Months	Sales	Expenses	Totals
3	Jan	120	115	
4	Feb	195	100	
5	Mar	230	125	
6				
7	Totals			
8				
9				

Figure 1-4: *The completed worksheet.*

1. Using Figure 1-4 as a guide, **finish entering the data in the worksheet.**

TOPIC C

Edit Data

After you enter the text and numeric data in your worksheet, you may find that you need to make some changes to that data. In this topic, you will edit existing data.

So, you're feeling great because you've entered all the text and numeric data for your worksheet. However, you take a closer look at the data and realize that you need to make some changes to it. Knowing how to edit your worksheet is an important step toward the end result—a complete worksheet that's correct, is easy to read, and looks good.

Navigating Among Cells

There are a number of ways to move around in Excel. To move to a specific cell or range (group of cells), you can use the mouse or the keyboard. Table 1-2 describes navigating in Excel using the mouse, and Table 1-3 describes navigating in Excel using the keyboard.

Table 1-2: *Using the Mouse*

Technique	Action
Click on the vertical scroll arrows	To move the worksheet display up or down one row per click.
Click on the horizontal scroll arrows	To move the worksheet display left or right one column per click.
Click the mouse button while pointing to the horizontal or vertical scroll arrows	To continuously move the worksheet display horizontally or vertically.
Click on a scroll bar, between the scroll box and the scroll arrow	To move the worksheet display one screen at a time.
Drag the scroll boxes	To move rapidly, either vertically or horizontally, through the worksheet area.
Click in the Name text box, type the cell reference, and press [Enter]	To move to the cell specified in the cell reference.

Table 1-3: *Using the Keyboard*

Technique	Action
Press the arrow keys	To move the active cell one cell at a time to the left, right, up, or down.
Press [Home]	To move the active cell to column A of the current row.
Press [Page Down] or [Page Up]	To move the active cell down or up by one screen's worth of rows.
Press [Tab]	To move the active cell to the right, one cell at a time.
Press [Shift][Tab]	To move the active cell to the left, one cell at a time.
Press [Ctrl][Home]	To move the active cell to A1 in the active worksheet.
Press [Alt][Page Up] or [Alt][Page Down]	To move the active cell one screen to the left or right, respectively.

Edit Data

Procedure Reference: Change an Entry Before You Enter it into a Cell

When you're entering data in a cell, what happens if you type some information into a cell incorrectly? If you haven't pressed [Enter], you can change the entry. This feature can save you time when editing your worksheets. To change an entry before you enter it into a cell, you can complete either of the following two choices:

1. Press [Backspace] to delete individual characters.

2. Press [Esc] or click the Cancel button (the X in the Formula bar) to clear the entire entry.

Procedure Reference: Change an Entry After You Enter it into a Cell

If you've already entered the data in the cell, you can still change it by completing either of the following three choices:

1. Double-clicking on the cell. This places you in Edit mode, where you can edit the text in the cell.

2. Press [F2]. This also places you in Edit mode, where you can edit the text in the cell.

3. Typing in the new text or data.

ACTIVITY 1-4

Editing Data

Setup:

If you did not finish the Completing the Worksheet activity at the end of the "Entering Data in a Worksheet" topic, open the file Worksheet Complete and use it to continue on with this lesson.

Scenario:

You have entered the basic data for your worksheet. However, after taking a closer look at what you've entered, you notice that some of the data needs to be changed. In this activity, you will replace the word Totals with Profits, the number 100 with 154, and the abbreviated months with the full month names.

What You Do	How You Do It
1. **In column D, replace the word Totals with the word Profits.**	a. **Select cell D2.** It currently contains the word Totals.
	b. **Type *Profits*.** Excel displays the new text in the Formula bar and in the cell.

c. **Press [Enter].** The word Profits replaces the word Totals, and cell D3 is now the active cell.

C	D
Expenses	Profits
115	
100	

2. **Replace the number 100 with the number 154.**

a. **Select cell C4.**

b. **Type** *154*.

c. **Press [Enter].** The number 154 replaces the number 100. Cell C5 is the active cell.

Now, let's use a different method for editing text.

3. **Use [F2] to change the word Jan to January.**

a. **Select cell A3.**

b. **Press [F2].** The mode indicator reads Edit. The insertion point appears after the letter n in the word Jan.

c. **Type** *uary* to complete the word.

d. **Press [Enter]** to enter the edited text.

4. **Use [F2] to change the word Feb to February.**

a. **Verify that cell A4 is selected.**

b. **Use the keyboard shortcut to change Feb to February and enter the change.**

5. **Use [F2] to change the word Mar to March.**

a. **Verify that cell A5 is selected.**

b. **Use the keyboard shortcut to change Mar to March and enter the change.**

	A	
1		
2	Months	Sa
3	January	
4	February	
5	March	
6		

TOPIC D

Change the Appearance of Data

Once all your data is entered in your worksheet, you might want to change its appearance. In this topic, you will change the appearance of data by using formatting.

Suppose you have all the data entered into a worksheet. However, when you look at the worksheet, it seems to be missing something. The data is correct, but its appearance is drab. You want to emphasize some of that data to make it easier to read and catch the reader's attention. Imagine what a worksheet would be like without formatting! Figure 1-5 displays the difference between unformatted and formatted data.

	A	B	C	D
1				
2	Months	Sales	Expenses	Profits
3	January	120	115	
4	February	195	154	
5	March	230	125	
6				
7	Totals			

	A	B	C	D
1				
2	**Months**	**Sales**	**Expenses**	**Profits**
3	*January*	120	115	
4	*February*	195	154	
5	*March*	230	125	
6				
7	***Totals***			

Figure 1-5: *Unformatted data (on the left) vs. formatted data (on the right).*

What is a Range?

Definition

A *range* is a rectangular group of adjacent cells in a worksheet.

Example

Some examples of ranges, including the following, are selected in Figure 1-6.

- A1:D2
- A5:A10
- C7:F12

Figure 1-6: *Selected ranges.*

Working with Ranges

Before you change text appearance, it's beneficial to know how to select a range.

To select a range of cells, you can use any of the following methods:

- With the mouse pointer, point to the center of the cell in one corner of the range; press and hold the mouse button while dragging to the opposite corner of the range; and release the mouse button.

- Select one corner of the range; press and hold the [Shift] key; and click on the opposite corner of the range to select all cells in between.

- Using only the keyboard, select one corner of the range; press and hold the [Shift] key; and press the arrow keys to highlight the range.

Adjacent vs. Non-adjacent Ranges

In Excel, you can select more than one range at the same time. However, those ranges do not have to be adjacent. For example, you can select the range A1:D2, press [Ctrl], and select the range A5:D6. To select a group of separate (non-adjacent) ranges that you want to affect at the same time, select the first range; press and hold the [Ctrl] key; and select the next range.

What is Formatting?

Definition

Formatting changes the way that numbers and text appear in a worksheet.

Example

For example, suppose you want to bold the text in cell A1. You would select cell A1, and click the Bold button on the Formatting toolbar to apply the bold attribute to the text in cell A1. Figure 1-7 displays a sample of unformatted and bold text.

	A	B
1		
2	Months	**Sales**

Figure 1-7: *Unformatted text vs. bold text.*

Adaptive Toolbars

Excel 2002 includes *adaptive toolbars*, which display toolbar buttons dynamically. The application keeps track of which buttons you use most often and displays these buttons on the toolbar, while hiding the least used buttons under the Toolbar Options arrow. Whenever you use the Toolbar Options list to click a button that doesn't currently appear on a toolbar, that button is then placed on the appropriate toolbar, and it displaces an unused (or least recently used) button. This creates a customized, or adaptive, environment. For example, if you frequently insert charts and you rarely bold text, the Insert Chart button appears on the Standard toolbar and the Bold button is placed in the Toolbar Options list. You can disable this feature (to appear more like Excel 97) by choosing Tools→Customize and then selecting the Options tab. Uncheck the first two check boxes, Show Standard And Formatting Toolbars On Two Rows and Always Show Full Menus.

Change the Appearance of Data

Procedure Reference: Change the Appearance of Data in a Worksheet

To change the appearance of data in your worksheet:

1. Select the cell or range of cells that you want to format.

2. Use the Formatting toolbar or Format menu to apply the desired formatting.

 Usually, you apply only one format for emphasis. Otherwise, you may clutter the appearance of your data with too many formats.

Format Painter

Once you have achieved a desired appearance for a cell, you can use the Format Painter to apply that format to other cells in the worksheet. To do so:

1. Select the cell that contains the format you desire.

2. To apply the format to a single cell or a range of cells:

   a. On the Formatting toolbar, click the Format Painter button.

   b. Click on the cell or range of cell to which you want to apply the formatting and press [Enter].

3. To apply the format to multiple cells not in a range:

   a. On the Formatting toolbar, double-click the Format Painter button

   b. Click on each cell to which you want to apply the formatting.

   c. When finished, click the Format Painter button to turn it off.

The Move Handle

The move handle serves as a dividing line between the docked toolbars. When the mouse pointer is over it, the mouse pointer becomes a four-headed arrow. You can drag the move handle to the left or to the right to resize any docked toolbar that shares a row with another docked toolbar. You drag the move handle back to put the move handle in its original position.

ACTIVITY 1-5

Changing the Appearance of Data

Scenario:

Your text and data is entered in your worksheet. You would like to apply formatting like that shown in Figure 1-8 so that your worksheet is visually appealing and easier to read.

	A	B	C	D
1				
2	**Months**	**Sales**	**Expenses**	**Profits**
3	*January*	120	115	
4	*February*	195	154	
5	*March*	230	125	
6				
7	*Totals*			

Figure 1-8: *The formatted data.*

What You Do	**How You Do It**

 Because Excel includes adaptive menus and toolbars, what appears on your screen as you key through this course may differ from the screen shots in this course.

 The buttons that appear on the Toolbars Options list are the less commonly used buttons. Once you use a button from a Toolbars Options list, it then appears on its main toolbar.

1. **Identify the following elements:**
   - Standard toolbar.
   - Formatting toolbar.
   - Move handle on the Standard and Formatting toolbars.
   - Buttons on the Standard Docked toolbar.

    You can use ScreenTips to identify the buttons on the toolbars.

2. **Underline the number 230, and observe the results.**

   a. **Select cell B5.**

   b. On the Formatting toolbar, **click the Underline button** U to underline the text.

c. **Deselect the text** to observe the results.

<u>230</u>

Also, notice that the Underline button appears with a light blue background and border, indicating that it is selected.

3. **Remove the Underline attribute from the number 230.**

a. **Select cell B5.**

b. On the Formatting toolbar, **click the Underline button.** Excel removes the Underline attribute.

Now, let's bold some text.

4. **Bold the column heading text.**

a. **Place the mouse pointer in the center of cell A2.**

b. **Press and hold the mouse button. Drag across until Excel selects cell D2.**

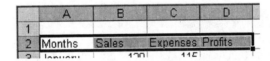

 The active cell is white. If you typed something, it would appear in the active cell.

c. **Release the mouse button.** Excel selects cells A2:D2. The selected cells are a cell range.

d. On the Formatting toolbar, **click the Bold button** **B** . Excel applies the bold attribute to the cells in the selected range.

Now, let's italicize some text.

5. **Apply the italic attribute to the month text.**

a. **Select cells A3:A5.**

b. On the Formatting toolbar, **click the Italic button** I. Excel applies the italic attribute to the cells in the selected range.

2	Months	Sal
3	*January*	
4	*February*	
5	*March*	
6		

6. **Apply the italic and bold attributes to the word Totals.**

   a. **Select cell A7.**

   b. **Click the Bold and Italic buttons.**

TOPIC E

Save a Workbook

Now that your worksheet is complete, you will want to save it. In this topic, you will save a workbook for the first time.

Let's say you're satisfied with this completed worksheet. However, it hasn't been saved yet. It only exists in temporary memory. If you don't save it, it will be lost forever when you close Excel, or if something terrible happens, such as a power outage. Then, you'll have to create it again from scratch. Therefore, you need to save it.

Save As vs. Save

Definition

The Save As command allows you to save a file to a permanent storage location, such as your hard disk or a 3.5" disk, for the first time, to save the changes in a file with a different name (other than the one that appears in the title bar), in a different location, or in a different format.

The Save command allows you to update a previously saved file in its current location and using its current name. To update a file, click the Save button on the Standard toolbar, or choose File→Save.

After you save a file, the title bar displays the complete filename.

After you save a file for the first time, you should continue to save your work frequently. If something happens to the file in memory, you'll have a recent copy of the file on disk. This keeps your retyping to a minimum.

Example

When you're ready to save a file for the first time, you'll want to use the File→Save As command. You can also use the File→Save As command to save the changes in a file with a different name (other than the one that appears in the title bar), in a different location, or in a different format. By default, Excel saves files in C:\My Documents. However, you can save your file in a folder of your choice.

Adaptive Menus

For all the commands you can issue using toolbar buttons, you can also use Excel's menus to issue the same command. Excel 2002 has *adaptive menus,* which means that they change as you use them. Menu items are dynamic. The drop-down menus display only the most commonly used commands. All the menus expand when you pause, double-click on the menu's name, or click on the expand arrows located at the bottom of the short menu. For example, when you first open a menu, it appears in short form. Some choices don't appear. The menus in Excel 2002 extend to display less commonly used commands that contain a dark gray background in the button area of the menu command.

 Don't confuse the grayed-out menu choices on a menu with hidden choices, which have a dark gray background in the button area of the menu command. As in all Office applications, grayed-out menu choices mean that an option is unavailable. Office applications use 3-D effects to display the difference between visible and hidden menu choices.

Naming a File

Filenames can contain up to 255 characters—letters, numbers, and the following special characters are allowed: ! @ # % ( ) – _ { } ' ~ including spaces. You can make the filenames as descriptive as you like. By default, Excel saves all workbook files with an .xls extension.

Save a Workbook

Procedure Reference: Save a File with a New Name

To save a file with a new name:

1. Choose File→Save As from the menu.

2. If necessary, create a new folder or browse to the folder where you want to save the file.

3. Enter the name of your file in the File Name text box.

4. Click Save.

ACTIVITY 1-6

Saving a Workbook File

Scenario:

You've completed the worksheet for your boss. Now, all you need to do is save it. In this activity, you'll save a worksheet for the first time by using the Save As Command. You'll name the worksheet My Sales Report and save it to a newly created folder.

What You Do	How You Do It
1. **Identify the commands available on your adaptive File menu.**	a. **Choose File** to display the File menu. You can use the File menu to manage your files.
	b. **View the available options.** Excel doesn't display all of the menu options.
	c. **Notice the downward-pointing arrow at the bottom of the menu.** | ⌄ |
	It indicates that other menu choices are available, and you can display them.

 All of Excel's menus have similar short and full forms.

 The menu may have already expanded.

2. **Identify the full command list available.** All the menus expand when you pause, double-click on the menu's name, or click on the expand arrows located at the bottom of the short menu.	a. **Place the mouse pointer on the downward-pointing arrow at the bottom of the menu.** The menu expands to display all the File options.
	b. With the File menu still expanded, **point to Edit to display the Edit menu.**
	c. **Look at the menu.** The expanded Edit menu already appears, revealing all of the editing commands.
	Don't confuse the grayed-out menu choices on a menu with hidden choices, which have a dark gray background in the button area of the menu command. As in all Office applications, grayed-out menu choices mean that an option is unavailable. Office applications use 3D effects to display the difference between visible and hidden menu choices.

3. If you want to save the worksheet for the first time, will you use the Save or the Save As command?

---

4. **Save your file as My Sales Report in a new folder called Excel in the My Documents folder.**

    a. From the File menu, **choose Save As** to display the Save As dialog box.

        You can use this dialog box to save a file for the first time. You can use the selected default filename in the File Name text box, or you can enter your own.

        By default, Excel displays the My Documents folder. Suppose you want to create a new folder to save a particular workbook to. Let's try it.

    b. In the Save As dialog box, **click the Create New Folder button** to display the New Folder dialog box.

    c. In the Name text box, **type *Excel* and click OK.**

    d. **Type *My Sales Report* to name the file.** The default text in the File Name text box is replaced.

    e. **Click Save.** Excel saves a copy of the file in the My Documents\Excel folder. This allows you to continue working with the same file.

---

5. **Verify that the new filename appears in the title bar.**

    a. **Look at the title bar.** Excel displays the new filename.

        Since you're done with the My Sales Report file, let's close it.

---

6. **Close all open files.**

a. **Click the appropriate Close Window button** to close all open files.

Excel remains open.

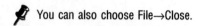 You can also choose File→Close.

TOPIC F

Obtain Help

Now that you know how to save a workbook file, you might want to take your next worksheet a step further. However, you're not quite sure how to perform a specific task in Excel. In this topic, you will use the Ask A Question box to obtain help.

So, your first Excel file is safely stored on the hard drive in the My Documents folder. You're ready to create your next worksheet, but this time, you want to take it a step further. Suppose you want to move and copy data, but you're not sure how to do it. You can use the Ask A Question box to enter your question and obtain possible answers to that question. Then, you'll know exactly how to accomplish your task in Excel.

Obtain Help

When you're working in Excel, there will be times when you'll need some additional assistance with a particular task.

Procedure Reference: Get Help in Excel

There are a number of ways to get help in Excel. To get help, choose from any of the following methods:

1. Press [F1].

2. Choose Help from the menu.

3. Click the Help button in a dialog box.

4. Use the Ask A Question box.

5. Use the Office Assistant.

The Office Assistant

The Office Assistant is an animated online aid that helps you use an application's Help system. The Office Assistant can answer your questions, offer tips, and provide help for a variety of features specific to Excel.

 When you start Excel 2002, the Office Assistant is hidden by default.

The Ask A Question Box

In Excel 2002, you can use the Ask A Question box to type a question without launching the Answer Wizard or the Office Assistant. To do so, simply click in the Ask A Question box that appears on the menu bar, type your question, and press [Enter]. Possible answers to your question are displayed in an Answer Wizard balloon even if the Office Assistant is turned off or hidden.

Context-sensitive Help

Of these possibilities, those that provide you with context-sensitive Help—which is sometimes referred to as Help, as you need it—are the [F1] key, the Help→What's This? menu command, Help buttons in dialog boxes, the Ask A Question Box, and the Office Assistant.

ACTIVITY 1-7

Obtaining Help

Setup:

No files are open.

Scenario:

Suppose you create a new worksheet and enter all the data. Then, you take a closer look at the worksheet and find that you want to move some of the data to other cells. You're not quite sure how to move data, so you decide to use the Ask A Question box to find the answer. In this activity, you will use a Help feature in Excel to obtain help on a task that you're unsure how to accomplish.

What You Do	How You Do It
1. Use the Ask A Question box to **ask the question** *How do you move data?*	a. On the right side of the menu bar, **identify the Ask A Question box.**

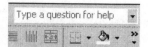

A prompt appears within the box asking you to type a question for help.

b. **Click in the Ask A Question box and type** *How do you move data?*

c. **Press [Enter].** An Answer Wizard balloon is displayed with a list of topics.

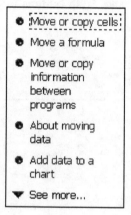

2. Display the contents of the first topic, Move Or Copy Cells.

a. At the top of the balloon, **place the mouse pointer over the text Move Or Copy Cells.** The mouse pointer changes to a hand. This indicates that the words are a hypertext link.

b. **Click on Move Or Copy Cells.** The Help window appears on the right side of the screen. Excel displays more choices.

Move or copy cells

Moving and copying cells

▶ Move or copy cells

▶ Insert moved or copied cells between existing cells

▶ Copy only visible cells

Moving and copying cell data

▶ Move or copy cell contents

▶ Copy cell values

▶ Copy cell formats

▶ Copy formulas

Note To cancel the moving border after you finish copying, press ESC.

You want to move and copy cell data.

3. Display the contents of the subtopic Move Or Copy Cell Contents.

a. **Click on the Move Or Copy Cell Contents hyperlink** to display the contents of that topic. Help lists the associated steps.

4. Close the Microsoft Excel Help window.

a. **Click the Close button.**

Lesson 1 Follow-up

In this lesson, you learned how to create a basic worksheet. You entered and edited data, changed text appearance, and saved a workbook. Then, you used Help to increase your knowledge of an Excel feature. You've passed the first major step for creating worksheets in Excel. Congratulations!

1. **How will you use Excel in your job?**

2. **What skills did you learn in this lesson that will be of most use to you when using Excel in your job?**

NOTES

LESSON 2
Editing Your Worksheet

Lesson Objectives:

In this lesson, you will work with cells and cell data by using a variety of moving and copying techniques.

You will:

*   Move data to other cells.

*   Copy data to other cells.

*   Use the AutoFill feature to fill cells with a series of data.

*   Insert and delete rows and columns.

*   Use the Undo and Redo commands.

*   Find and replace numbers.

*   Enter numbers in a selected range.

*   Use the Text to Speech toolbar to verify worksheet data.

Introduction

In the previous lesson, you created a basic worksheet. After you create a worksheet, you'll undoubtedly want to make editing changes to modify or add to the data it contains. In this lesson, you'll make various editing changes to a worksheet.

You're sitting at your desk basking in the glory of having completed the worksheet for your boss ahead of schedule. You're thinking, "I'm glad that worksheet is done," feeling very relieved. Suddenly, someone taps you on the shoulder...no, it couldn't be him. You turn around...it's him! What does he want now? You guessed it–changes to the worksheet! Ugh!!!

TOPIC A

Moving Data to Other Cells

One of the skills you'll use to edit data in your worksheet is moving data. In this topic, you will open an existing workbook for editing and move data to other cells.

You've entered text and numeric data in a worksheet. You review what you've entered, and you realize you entered text in the wrong location. Instead of deleting and retyping that data in the correct location, you can save time by moving the data to its new location.

Task Panes

Definition

You might have noticed that when you first open Excel 2002, a new pane is displayed on the right side of the application window. This new pane is called a task pane. A *task pane* is a window that allows you to easily access frequently used commands. As you're working in Excel, you'll notice that the task pane is automatically displayed when you perform a frequently used command.

Example

For example, when you open Excel for the first time, the New Workbook task pane is displayed, providing you with options such as opening an existing workbook or creating a new blank workbook. These are tasks that you would want to perform as soon as you open Excel. You can also use task panes to view the contents of the clipboard, search, and insert clip art.

Move Data to Other Cells

After you open a worksheet, you can make editing changes to it. You can move and copy data among worksheets, workbooks, or other applications.

Procedure Reference: Move Data

When you move data, Excel removes the cell contents and pastes them in another location. When you paste the contents of cells, you overwrite the existing cell contents. To move data:

1.   Select the data.

2. Once the data is selected, you can use any of the following methods to move it:

- Choose Edit→Cut, select the destination, and choose Edit→Paste. (Or, from the shortcut menu, choose the Cut and Paste commands.)

- Click the Cut button, select the destination, and click the Paste button.

- Place the mouse pointer at an edge of the selection, drag (press and hold the mouse button) to the new destination, and drop the selection (release the mouse button).

> You can't use the drag-and-drop method of copying to move data between different worksheets.

ACTIVITY 2-1

Moving Data to Other Cells

Objective:

Move the data to other cells by dragging.

Data Files:

- Editing

Scenario:

You're ready to make the changes to the worksheet that your boss has requested. Your first change is to move around in your worksheet. In this activity, you will move the heading Totals one cell to the left and the date text for the Northeastern Region one cell to the left.

What You Do	How You Do It

1. Use the New Workbook task pane to preview and open the Editing file in the My Documents folder.

 You can also click the Open button.

a. If necessary, **choose View→Task Pane** to display the New Workbook task pane.

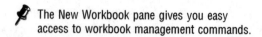 The New Workbook pane gives you easy access to workbook management commands.

b. In the New Workbook task pane under Open A Workbook, **click on More Workbooks.**

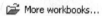 More workbooks...

The Open dialog box is displayed.

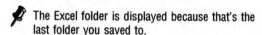 The Excel folder is displayed because that's the last folder you saved to.

c. **Click the Up One Level button** 📁 . **The contents of My Documents is displayed.**

d. **Preview the file to verify it's the correct one by clicking the downward-pointing arrow next to the Views button** 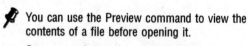 **and choosing Preview. Excel displays a preview of the selected file in the right pane.**

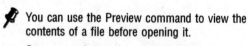 You can use the Preview command to view the contents of a file before opening it.

Once you select a view, that view remains active until you select another one.

e. **Select Editing and click Open** to open the file.

2. Move the heading text Totals one cell to the left from H4 to G4.

a. **Select cell H4.**

b. **Position the mouse pointer over the border of cell H4.** The mouse pointer changes to an arrow and displays a four-headed arrow.

Excel 2002: Level 1

c. **Press and hold the mouse button. Drag to cell G4.**

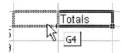

 A ScreenTip appears indicating the destination cell.

d. **Release the mouse button.** Excel moves the text Totals to cell G4.

3. **Move the date text for the North-eastern Region one cell to the left from B2 to A2.**

   a. **Select cell B2.**

   b. **Position the mouse pointer over the border of cell B2.**

   c. **Press and hold the mouse button. Drag to cell A2.**

   d. **Release the mouse button.** The date text now appears in cell A2.

	A
1	**Books and Be**
2	5/15/2002

4. **Save the file as *My Editing*.**

   a. **Display the Save As dialog box.**

   b. **In the File Name text box, type *My Editing*.**

   c. **Click Save.**

TOPIC B

Copy Data to Other Cells

Moving data is one method for getting data from one area of your worksheet to another. Copying is another. In this topic, you'll copy data to other cells.

You've entered information in your worksheet and decide you want to use the same data in another area. The move feature won't help you because that deletes the data from the original location. You want it to appear in both the original location and the new location. Instead of typing the same data in the new location, you can use the copy feature to save you time.

Smart Tags

Definition

When you're copying data in a worksheet, you will encounter smart tags. A *smart tag* is a button that appears when you perform an action or error, such as pasting data, that gives you options related to the action or error.

Example

You will encounter a variety of smart tags while working in Excel 2002, including the Paste Options smart tag (shown in Figure 2-1). For example, if you select cell A1, click the Copy button, select cell A15, and choose the Paste button, the Paste Options smart tag will appear below the pasted data.

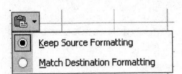

Figure 2-1: *The Paste Options smart tag.*

The Paste Options button then allows you to select one of the following options:

- Keep Source Formatting.
- Match Destination Formatting.
- Values And Number Formatting.
- Keep Source Column Widths.
- Formatting Only.
- Link Cells.

Other common smart tags you might encounter while working with Excel are the AutoCorrect Options smart tag and Automatic Layout Options smart tag.

Copy Data to Other Cells

Procedure Reference: Copy Data

In addition to moving data, you can copy data in a worksheet. When you copy data, Excel copies the cell contents and pastes them in another location. To copy data:

1. Select the data.

2. Once the data is selected, you can use any of the following methods to copy it:

- Choose Edit→Copy, select the destination, and choose Edit→Paste.

> 🖈 You can also choose the Copy and Paste commands from the shortcut menu.

- Click the Copy button, select the destination, and click the Paste button.
- Point to the border of the cell range, while pressing the [Ctrl] key, drag to the new location, and release the mouse button and then the [Ctrl] key..
- Drag the fill handle on the selection to the adjacent cells to which you want to copy the data and release the mouse button.

> 🖈 You'll learn more about the fill handle in the next topic.

ACTIVITY 2-2

Copying Data to Other Cells

Objective:
Copy text using different techniques.

Setup:
My Editing is open.

Scenario:
Your boss likes the way you've set up the worksheet. He wants to have a totals column in the Mideastern Region just like you have it in the Northeastern region. You already know how to move data. The steps for copying data are very similar. In this activity, you will copy data to other cells.

What You Do	How You Do It
1. **Use the Copy and Paste command to copy the word Totals from the Northeastern Region data to the same location in the Mideastern Region data.**	a. **Select cell G4.** You're going to copy the word Totals to cell O4.
	b. On the Standard toolbar, **click the Copy button** [icon] . A marquee surrounds the selected cell.
	c. **Select cell O4.**
	d. On the Standard toolbar, **click the Paste button** [icon] . Excel copies the text Totals to cell O4.
	🖈 A smart tag appears below cell O4.

2. **Display the Paste Options drop-down list and observe the paste options.**

a. **Click the Paste Options drop-down arrow** to display the Paste Options drop-down list.

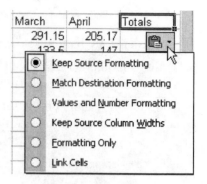

The list includes different formatting options for pasting the copied information into your worksheet.

b. **Look at the paste options.** You want to keep the source formatting.

3. **Close the Paste Options drop-down list without making changes.**

a. **Select Keep Source Formatting** to close the drop-down list without making changes (or click on the Paste Options drop-down list).

4. Drag the ID heading and its accompanying four IDs to cells B16:B20, and save the changes to the file.

a. **Select cells B4:B8.**

b. **Press and hold [Ctrl]. Point to the border of cell B8.** The mouse pointer changes to an arrow with a plus sign (+).

c. **Press and hold the mouse button. Drag to select cell B16** to copy the ID title and four IDs to cells B16:B20.

> As you're dragging, a ScreenTip appears to guide you to the correct destination.

d. **Release the mouse button. Release [Ctrl].** Excel copies the text.

> ⚠ If you release [Ctrl] first, the selected data will be moved, not copied.

e. On the Standard toolbar, **click the Save button** 🖫 to save the changes to the file with the same name and location.

TOPIC C

Fill Cells with a Series of Data

You've learned you can copy identical data from one location to another. In this topic, you'll learn how to copy data from one location to another and alter its value just slightly.

Have you ever needed to enter a series of data in a worksheet, such as the days of the week or the months of the year? If so, you probably noticed that it can be a time-consuming task. When entering data, you always run the risk of entering incorrect data. Well, if you want to save time, you can now use the AutoFill feature. It allows you to enter data in one cell to establish a pattern and drag to fill other cells without having to key in any additional information.

AutoFill

Definition

The *AutoFill* feature allows you to fill a selected range of cells with a series of data. You enter data in one or more cells and drag to fill other cells without having to key in any additional information. Excel makes some assumptions when you enter the starting value(s) for the series you want to fill the cells with. Depending on the type of data you're entering (text or numeric), you may only have to enter data in one cell for Excel to interpret the type of series you want to fill.

Example

For example, you can fill cells with dates, numbers, and text/number combinations.

Fill Handle

You can use the fill handle to copy data. The *fill handle* is the box at the corner of a cell or range that you can use to activate Excel's AutoFill feature. When a cell or range of cells contains data that you can display in increments, drag the fill handle to the left, right, up, or down to fill a range with data.

Fill Cells with a Series of Data

Procedure Reference: Fill Cells with a Series of Data

To fill cells with a series of data:

1. Enter the first value or first two values in your data series in a cell.

2. Select the cell.

3. Drag the selection's fill handle as far as you want cells filled with the data.

4. Release the mouse button. Excel fills the range with the appropriate data, continuing the pattern that you began with your first entry.

ACTIVITY 2-3

Filling Cells with a Series of Data

Setup:
My Editing is open.

Scenario:
Now you're ready to add some new data for January through April and for all four quarters in your worksheet. You need to enter the headings for each month and all four quarters. You decide to use the AutoFill feature to save time and reduce typing mistakes.

What You Do	How You Do It
1. Enter *January* in cell C16.	a. Select cell C16.
	b. Type *January* and press [Enter].
2. Use the AutoFill feature to fill the three cells to the right of January with February, March, and April, respectively.	a. Select cell C16.
	b. Place the insertion point on the fill handle. It's the black square that appears on the lower-right corner of the selected cell, cell C16.

The insertion point changes to a thin black cross.

c. **Drag the fill handle to cell F16.** As you drag across, Excel displays the months of the year. Excel automatically fills the selected cells with the months of the year.

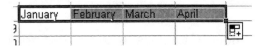

The Auto Fill Options button is also displayed.

3.   Identify the options provided by the Auto Fill Options button.

_____

4.   Enter *Qtr. 1* in cell C26.

   a.   Select cell C26.

   b.   Type *Qtr. 1* and press [Enter].

5.   Use the AutoFill feature to fill the three cells to the right of Qtr. 1 with Qtr. 2, Qtr. 3, and Qtr. 4, respectively.

   a.   Select cell C26.

   b.   Place the insertion point on the fill handle.

   c.   Drag the fill handle to cell F26.

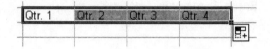

6.   Identify the options provided by the AutoFill Options button for the Qtr series.

TOPIC D

Insert and Delete Rows and Columns

Another aspect of editing your worksheet data is to add or delete entire rows or columns to your worksheet.

You've made a number of changes to your worksheet. You're looking at it and realize that you've missed some data and need to add a few more rows of information near the top. You could use your move skills to move the data down, but there's an easier way to complete this task. You can insert and delete rows and columns without having to move existing data. In this topic, you'll learn how to insert and delete both rows and columns.

Insert and Delete Rows and Columns

Procedure Reference: Insert or Delete Entire Rows or Columns

Adding a row or column to your worksheet inserts a blank row or column within your worksheet and moves all existing data down or to the right. To insert or delete entire rows or columns:

1.   Select one or more rows or columns.

2. Right-click on the selected rows or columns.

3. Choose Insert or Delete from the shortcut menu.

Selecting Rows and Columns

The first step when inserting or deleting a row or column is to select a row or column in the worksheet. There are different selection techniques that you can use when inserting and deleting rows and columns.

- To select an entire column or row, click on the column or row heading (column letter or row number).
- To select a group of columns or rows, drag across the headings.
- To select nonadjacent columns or rows, press [Ctrl] when clicking on the column or row headings after the first column or row is selected.

ACTIVITY 2-4

Inserting and Deleting Rows and Columns

Setup:

My Editing is open.

Scenario:

Believe it or not, there are still more changes to be made to the worksheet. Your boss is unhappy with the spacing in the worksheet. He wants you to insert two rows at the top of the worksheet, a column before columns A and I, and a row between the heading text and the individual sales data to make the data look less crowded.

What You Do	How You Do It
1. Insert two rows above row 1.	a. Drag down through the headings for rows 1 and 2 to select two rows across the entire worksheet.

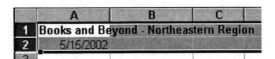

b. **Right-click on the selected area and choose Insert.** Excel inserts two rows above the selected rows.

Let's insert another row.

2. **Insert a row between rows 8 and 9.**

a. **Select the row heading for row 9.**

b. **Right-click on the selected area and choose Insert.** Excel inserts a row. Row 9 is now blank.

3. **What was the effect on the Northeastern Region and Mideastern Region data?**

4. **Delete row 9.**

a. **Verify that row 9 is selected.**

b. **Right-click on row 9 and choose Delete.** Excel deletes the row. Now, let's insert a column.

5. **Insert a column before column A.**

a. **Select the column heading for column A.**

b. **Right-click on the selected column and choose Insert.** Excel inserts a new column.

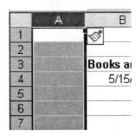

PRACTICE ACTIVITY 2-5

Inserting Additional Rows and Columns

Activity Time:

5 minutes

Scenario:

You need to insert a few more rows and columns.

1. **Insert a column between columns H and I.**

2. **Insert a row between rows 6 and 7.**

3. **Save the file.**

Inserting and Deleting Selected Cells

In addition to adding or deleting columns or rows to your worksheets, you can also add or delete blank cells. To do so:

1. Select a range of cells.

2. Right-click on the selected cells.

3. Indicate whether you wish to insert or delete cells by choosing either Insert or Delete from the shortcut menu.

4. If inserting cells, choose one of the following from the Insert dialog box:

    • Shift Cells Right—to shift the contents of the cells to the right when you insert cells.

    • Shift Cells Down—to shift the contents of the cells down when you insert cells.

- Entire Row—to insert an entire row when you insert cells.

- Entire Column—to insert an entire column when you insert cells.

If deleting cells, choose one of the following from the Delete dialog box:

- Shift Cells Left—to shift the contents of the remaining cells to the left when you delete cells.

- Shift Cells Up—to shift the contents of the remaining cells up when you delete cells.

- Entire Row—to delete an entire row when you delete cells.

- Entire Column—to delete an entire column when you delete cells.

5. Click OK.

 To delete the contents of a cell, select the cell(s), and either choose Edit→Clear→Contents or simply press the [Delete] key.

ACTIVITY 2-6

Inserting and Deleting Selected Cells

Scenario:

Upon closer review, you believe that you entered the monthly figures for Books and Beyond under the wrong column headings. To fix this, you use the Insert Cells command to insert blank cells in the range M8:M11, shifting the cells in the current range M8:M11 to the right. You then realize that they were, in fact, correctly entered; so you delete the blank cells.

What You Do	How You Do It
1. Insert blank cells in the range M8:M11.	a. Select cells M8:M11.
	b. Right-click on the selected area and choose Insert to display the Insert dialog box.

c. Click OK.

2.   What occurred as a result of inserting the blank cells?

_____

3.   Delete the blank cells in the range M8:M11.

a. If necessary, **select cells M8:M11.**

b. **Right-click on the selected area and choose Delete.** The Delete dialog box is displayed.

c. **Click OK** to shift the range N8:Q11 to the left.

TOPIC E

Undo and Redo an Entry

While working on a worksheet in Excel, you might perform an action and then want to go back and reverse what you just did. In those instances, you can use the Undo and Redo commands to reverse your actions. In this topic, you will use those commands.

Have you ever deleted data in Excel or another software application and wished there was a way to undo your deletion? Fortunately, you can use the Undo button to return that data to your worksheet without having to re-key it. Likewise, if you use the Undo command and then change your mind, you can use the Redo command.

The Undo and Redo Features

Undo allows you to reverse one or more of your most recent actions. Redo allows you to cancel one or more of your most recent actions.

 Not all actions can be undone in Excel. For example, you can't undo a File→Save. Also once you save a file, you can't undo things you did before the save.

Suppose you're clearing the contents of a cell, and you realize you deleted the wrong data. You can use the Undo command to reverse your last action. What if you undo a command and you change your mind? For example, you enter some text in a cell, you press Undo because you decide you don't want that text, and then you realize that you really do. You can use the Redo command to cancel your last undo action.

Undo and Redo an Entry

Procedure Reference: Use the Undo and Redo Commands

You can use the Undo command to reverse your last action and the Redo command to cancel your last undo.

1.   To reverse your last action, click the Undo button (or choose Edit→Undo).

2.   To cancel your last undo action, click the Redo button (or choose Edit→Redo).

The Edit, Clear Command

While working with worksheets, you will at some point have to delete information from cells. Excel offers you several options for deleting cell content. To delete the contents of a cell, and not the cell itself, select the cell and choose Edit→Clear→Contents. You can also choose to delete selected cell contents by simply pressing the [Delete] key on the keyboard. In addition to the deleting cell contents, the Edit→Clear command offers three other options:

- Choose Edit→Clear→All to clear formats, contents, and any comments in or applied to a cell. (Comments are notes that you enter for a cell using the Insert→Comment command.)

- Choose Edit→Clear→Formats to clear any formats applied to a cell.

- Choose Edit→Clear→Comments to clear any comments applied to a cell.

ACTIVITY 2-7

Using the Undo and Redo Commands

Setup:

If you did not complete Activity 2-5 in Topic 2D, open the file, Editing Complete, and use it to continue on with this lesson. My Editing is open.

Scenario:

Another change that your boss needs you to make to the worksheet is to clear a range of data. You select the data and delete it. You then realize you deleted the wrong data, so you use the Undo button to reverse your deletion. A short time later, your boss appears at your desk, and tells you that he made a mistake. He actually wants the data you just deleted. You use the Redo button to cancel your last action.

What You Do	How You Do It
1. Clear the headings Qtr. 1 through Qtr. 4.	a. Select cells D29:G29.
	b. Press [Delete] to delete the contents of the selected cells.
	You just realize that you deleted the wrong content.
	To delete the contents of a cell, you can also select the cell and choose Edit→Clear→Contents.

2. **Undo the deletion of the quarter headings.**

   a. On the Standard toolbar, **click the Undo button** ⟲ ▾ . Excel returns the deleted text to the selected cells.

      Suppose your boss comes to your desk and tells you he wants the data in cells D29:G29 deleted after all.

3. **Use the Redo command to delete the quarter headings.**

   a. On the Standard toolbar, **click the Redo button** ⟳ ▾ to clear the contents of cells D29:G29.

4. **Identify the contents of the Undo history drop-down list.**

   Do you think you can you undo more than one action at once?

TOPIC F

Find and Replace Numbers

The first part of editing your data is finding that data within your worksheet. So far in this lesson, you have scanned the worksheet and visually identified the data. In this topic, you will use Excel's Find and Replace feature to locate and change that incorrect data.

You just realized that a piece of data in your worksheet is incorrect. You aren't sure where the data is located in the worksheet. You could search for the data manually by visually examining each cell starting from the beginning of the worksheet, but that would take a lot of time. Instead, you decide to use the Find and Replace feature to find and replace the incorrect value with the correct value. In large worksheets, it will be quicker than doing it manually, and if there happens to be any other instances of the same piece of data that you didn't know about, you can change their value at the same time.

Find and Replace

You might find an instance where you inserted specific text or a number in one or more cells in a worksheet, and you need to change it. The Edit→Replace command allows you to have Excel search for cells containing specific text or numbers within your worksheet and replace the cell's contents with a new value.

Find and Replace Numbers

Procedure Reference: Find and Replace Text or Numbers

To find and replace text or numbers:

1. To search the entire worksheet, select any single cell in the worksheet.

   To search a specific range of cells, select that range only.

2. Choose Edit→Replace to display the Find And Replace dialog box.

3. In the Find What text box, enter the text or number you want to search for.

4. In the Replace With text box, enter the text or number you want to replace the found text with.

5. Click Find Next.

6. To replace the selected occurrence of found characters, click Replace. To replace all occurrences of the found characters, click Replace All.

7. When you're done with the search, click Close to close the Find And Replace dialog box.

When you use the Find and Replace feature, you can set a number of different options depending on what you are finding and replacing. Those options include the following:

- You can find/replace data in the active worksheet or all worksheets within a workbook. The default is to find/replace within the active worksheet.

- You can find/replace by rows or columns. By rows is the default.

- You can look in formulas when you're finding/replacing data.

    You'll learn more about formulas in the next lesson.

- You can also look in values and comments when you're finding only. The default is to find/replace formulas.

- You can match case and/or match entire cell contents when you're finding and replacing data. Both options are turned off by default.

ACTIVITY 2-8

Finding and Replacing Numbers

Scenario:

Your boss just realized that one of the numbers in the worksheet is incorrect. He gave you the value 295.44 as the April sales figure for employee 789012345. The actual sale figure is 314.04. He wants the data fixed immediately. You decide to use Find And Replace because it will quickly locate all the values your boss wants you to change.

What You Do	How You Do It
1. Display the Find And Replace dialog box.	a. Verify that a single cell is selected.
	b. Choose Edit→Replace to display the Find And Replace dialog box. You're going to find and replace a specific number.
2. Search for the incorrect April sales figure for Employee 789012345 and replace 295.44 with the number 314.04.	a. In the Find What text box, **type 295.44 and press [Tab]** to move to the Replace With text box.
	b. In the Replace With text box, **type 314. 04.**

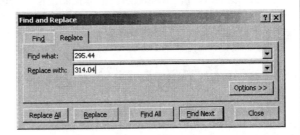

c. **Click Find Next.** Cell P10 is selected.

d. **Verify that this is the value that corresponds with the incorrect April sales figure for Employee 789012345.**

e. **Click Replace.** Excel replaces 295.44 with 314.04.

3. Find all other instances of 295.44 to verify that no other incorrect April sales data is recorded in the worksheet for Employee 789012345. Save the file.

a. **Click Find Next.** A message box is displayed indicating that Excel can't find the data you're searching for.

b. **Click OK** to clear the message.

c. **Click Close** to close the Find And Replace dialog box.

d. **Save the file.**

TOPIC G

Enter Data in a Range

In addition to entering data by navigating to and selecting each individual cell, you can enter data by selecting a range of cells and then navigate only within the range. In this topic, you will enter numbers in a selected range.

Have you ever been in a mode when entering data in a worksheet or other document, and suddenly realized that the insertion point was in the wrong place? By selecting the range first, the insertion point moves only within the selected range, eliminating the chance that the insertion point might end up in a cell where you don't want it.

Enter Data in a Range

Procedure Reference: Enter Data in a Range of Cells

You can select a range before you type data and limit the active cell to the boundaries of the selected range. When you enter data in a selected range, Excel allows you to enter data and change the position of the cell pointer within that range as indicated here:

1. Select a range of cells.

2. Type an entry in a cell within the selected range.

3. Navigate to the next cell in the range by:
   - Pressing [Enter], or clicking the Enter button, to move the active cell down the columns in the selected range, starting with the current column and moving to the right.
   - Pressing [Shift][Enter] to move the active cell up the columns in the selected range.
   - Pressing [Tab] to move the active cell across the rows in the selected range, starting with the current row and moving down.
   - Pressing [Shift][Tab] to move the active cell from right to left across the rows in the selected range.

If you use any arrow keys or the mouse to navigate within the selected range, you will deselect the range.

🖈 When the cell pointer reaches the lower-right corner of the range, you can move the active cell back to the upper-left corner of the range by pressing [Enter] or [Tab].

ACTIVITY 2-9

Entering Data in a Selected Range

Setup:

My Editing is open.

Scenario:

So, you're almost done making the changes to the worksheet that your boss has requested. One of the last tasks you need to accomplish is to enter the data for January and February for your first four IDs, as shown in Figure 2-2. Because your data is contained within a range, your coworker, who uses Excel on a regular basis, suggests that you select the range before entering the data to keep your active cell within the range making navigation and data entry easier and more accurate. This data is contained within the range D20:E23.

ID	January	February	M
123456789	200	175	
234567890	325	134	
345678901	130	98	
456789012	313	210	

Figure 2-2: *The completed range of data.*

What You Do	How You Do It
1. Using a selected range, **enter the data for January and February as shown in Figure 2-2 and save the file.**	a. **Select the range D20:E23.**
	b. In cell D20, **type** *200* **and press [Enter].**

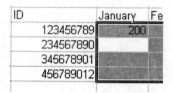

c. **Enter** *325* **in cell D21.**

d. **Using Figure 2-2 as a guide, enter the remaining numbers in the selected range.**

e. **Save the file.**

TOPIC H

Verify Data in a Range

Part of entering and editing data is checking that the data you entered is correct. In this topic, you will use the Text to Speech feature to check selected data.

Have you ever been in a meeting with a printout of an Excel worksheet and made changes to it? If you have, then you have also probably incorporated those changes into the electronic version of that worksheet. Sometimes, this checking process can be tedious, because worksheet fonts are often small and cumbersome because there are so many numbers. The Text to Speech feature allows you to easily check those entries with just a few quick steps. Before you know it, your data will be verified, and you will be assured of its accuracy.

Verify Data in a Range

Procedure Reference: Use the Text to Speech Toolbar

You can use the Text to Speech feature to audibly verify selected data. Excel provides you with the Text to Speech toolbar, which includes a number of tools you can use when you're verifying data. To do so:

1. Choose View→Toolbars→Text To Speech to display the Text To Speech toolbar.

2. Select the cells that you want to verify.

3. Choose how you want Excel to read back the data by clicking By Rows or By Columns on the Text To Speech toolbar.

4. On the Text To Speech toolbar, click Speak Cells to have Excel read back each cell in your selection.

5. If necessary, you can use the Stop Speaking button on the Text To Speech toolbar to stop the playback and correct an error.

Text to Speech Options

Before you verify selected data, you can click the By Rows or By Columns button to choose how you want the data to be verified. To verify data in a selected range, click the Speak Cells button. Each cell is highlighted as its contents are spoken. Whatever is visible in the cell is read. If you need to stop the verification during the process, simply click the Stop Speaking button. You can then continue verification by clicking the Speak Cells button again.

If desired, you can have the cells verified after you enter the data in each cell. Simply click the Speak On Enter button before you enter any of the data in the selected range. After you enter data in each cell, that data will be verified.

ACTIVITY 2-10

Verifying Data in a Range

Setup:

To use the Text to Speech feature, your computer must be equipped with a sound card and speakers. You don't need a microphone to use this feature. The file, My Editing, is displayed in the worksheet window. If you did not complete the Entering Data in a Selected Range activity at the end of Topic 2G, open the file, Verifying Complete, and use it to continue on with this lesson.

Scenario:

You're finally on the last step of all the editing changes your boss has requested. You just entered a group of numbers in a selected range. Now, you want to go back and verify the accuracy of those numbers. As you're verifying, you realize that the number in cell E21 is incorrect. So, you'll have to stop verifying, fix the number, and continue verifying.

What You Do	How You Do It
1. Display the Text To Speech toolbar, and use the ScreenTips to view the name of each button on the toolbar.	a. Choose View→Toolbars→Text To Speech. The Text To Speech toolbar is displayed.
	b. On the Text To Speech toolbar, **point to the first button.** The name of the button appears in a text box.
	c. **Point to the remaining buttons on the toolbar** to display the names.
2. On the Text To Speech toolbar, **set the option to have Excel read the data by column, and have Excel read back the contents of each cell up to the number 98.**	a. On the Text To Speech toolbar, **click the By Columns button** . The cells will be read by column.
	b. **Click the Speak Cells button** . Excel begins reading the contents of each cell.
	c. When the number 98 is selected, **click the Stop Speaking button** .
3. Replace the number 134 with 164.	a. **Press [Shift][Tab] twice** to return to cell E21.
	b. **Press [Backspace]** to remove the contents of cell E21.
	c. **Type** *164* **and press [Enter].**
4. Have Excel read the remaining data in the selection, and close the Text To Speech toolbar.	a. Click the Speak Cells button.
	✎ You can also choose View→Toolbars→Text To Speech.
	b. On the Text To Speech toolbar, **click the Close button.**
5. Save and close all open files.	a. Click the Save button.
	b. Click the Close Window button.

Lesson 2 Follow-up

In this lesson, you made some basic editing changes to your worksheet. You moved and copied data, filled cells with a series of data, inserted and deleted rows, columns, and cells, used the undo and redo features, and entered and verified data in a range. By making these editing changes, you obtained the skills you can use to quickly edit the content of your worksheets.

1. **What types of editing changes do you anticipate you will make to your worksheets?**

2. **Which editing skill did you learn that will be of the most use to you back at your office?**

NOTES

LESSON 3
Performing Calculations

Lesson Objectives:

In this lesson, you will perform calculations on data by using formulas, including functions.

You will:

- Create and enter a sum.
- Use a function to create a formula.
- Copy formulas.
- Create an absolute reference.

Introduction

Now that you know how to enter and edit data in your worksheet, you're ready to begin performing calculations on the data. In this lesson, you'll use the data you've already entered and perform calculations on it.

You might be thinking that it's going to be difficult to perform calculations on your data. You have visions of sitting down with your worksheet, a calculator, and manually adding, subtracting, multiplying, and dividing. However, by using formulas, you allow Excel to do the calculation work for you. Formulas are great because they save you time in calculating data and automatically update whenever you change the numbers in your worksheet.

TOPIC A

Sum a Range of Data

Your worksheet contains a lot of great numeric data, but it doesn't mean much if you don't calculate it to obtain specific results. In this topic, you will sum a range of data by creating a simple formula.

The data that's contained in your worksheet is good, but it will be more valuable to you and others if you perform calculations on it. By using formulas to calculate your data, you'll save time, and if you make any changes to the data, those changes will be reflected in the formulas. For example, you have to balance your personal checkbook on a regular basis, adding in deposits and subtracting withdrawals. If you make an error, you won't know it until you balance your checkbook. By using formulas in Excel, the calculations are automatic and free of calculation errors, even if you change a number or add new data to the formula.

Formulas

Definition

A *formula* is a set of instructions that you enter in a cell to perform calculations.

Example

For example, enter the number 350 in cell B1; enter the number 450 in B2; enter the formula =B1+B2 in cell B3. Excel displays the value 800 in cell B3. Any time that you change the value in cell B1 or B2, Excel recalculates the value of cell B3.

 You can create formulas by using numbers (for example, 350+450). However, it's preferable to construct formulas that refer to worksheet cells. In Excel, you create formulas by preceding the expressions with an equal sign (=).

Order of Operations

Definition

When you're examining or creating formulas, you should keep in mind that there's a specific sequence that Excel follows when it performs calculations. This sequence is known as the *order of operations* and it's performed as follows:

1. Parentheses: Computations enclosed in parentheses are performed first, no matter where they appear in the formula.

2. Exponents: Computations involving exponents are performed second.

3. Multiplication and division: Excel performs these operations next. Because they are equal with regard to the order in which Excel performs them, Excel performs them in the order in which it encounters them (from left to right).

4. Addition and subtraction: Excel performs these operations last. Excel also performs them in the order in which it encounters them (from left to right).

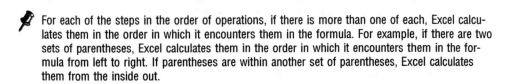 For each of the steps in the order of operations, if there is more than one of each, Excel calculates them in the order in which it encounters them in the formula. For example, if there are two sets of parentheses, Excel calculates them in the order in which it encounters them in the formula from left to right. If parentheses are within another set of parentheses, Excel calculates them from the inside out.

One way for you to remember the order of operations is through the mnemonic "Please Excuse My Dear Aunt Sally." The capitals in the mnemonic (PEMDAS) correspond to the names of the operations in their correct order.

Mathematical Symbols

When you're building formulas, use:

- The plus sign (+) for addition.
- The minus sign (–) for subtraction.
- The asterisk (*) for multiplication.
- The front slash (/) for division.
- The caret symbol (^) for exponents.
- The open and close parentheses ( ) to group computation instructions.

Example

Here's an example of a formula, followed by the order in which Excel would compute it:

=(A1 + B2) / 100 - C3 * D4^2

1. (A1 + B2)—The contents of cell A1 plus the contents of cell B2.

2. D4^2—The contents of cell D4 squared.

3. Step 1 / 100—The result of step 1 divided by 100.

4. C3 * step 2—The contents of cell C3 multiplied by the result of step 2.

5. Step 4 – step 3—The result of step 4 minus the result of step 3.

Sum a Range of Data

Procedure Reference: Enter a Formula

The steps for entering a formula are outlined here:

1. Select the cell where you want to enter the formula.

2. Type = (the equal sign).

3. Enter the appropriate cell references along with the mathematical symbols for performing your calculation(s).

When entering a formula, you can enter cell references or click on the desired cells. Clicking on the cells may eliminate typing errors and prevent mistakes as you determine the cell references by looking at them.

4. Press [Enter] or click the Enter button on the Formula bar.

You can use the Formula bar to enter or edit values or formulas in cells. It also displays the constant value or formula stored in the active cell.

AutoSum

Whenever you want to add the sum of all numbers in a contiguous row or column, you can use AutoSum. To do so:

1. Click on the empty cell directly below or to the right of the contiguous row or column of which you want to find the sum.

2. On the Standard toolbar, click the AutoSum button 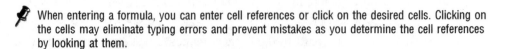 and press [Enter].

True vs. Displayed Cells Contents

If you're using formulas to calculate numbers, you'll find that you can't see the true contents of a cell just by looking at it. What you see is the number that Excel calculates as the results of the formula. To view the true contents of a cell, select the cell, and observe its contents in the formula bar.

Automatic Recalculation

Automatic recalculation updates the results of formulas containing cell references when you change the contents of the cell to which those formulas refer. For example:

Cell A1 contains the value 2.

Cell B1 contains the value 2.

Cell C1 contains the formula =A1+B1 displaying the value of 4.

If you change the value of cell A1 to 3, the formula in cell C1 is automatically recalculated and C1 updates to display the value 5.

Modifying a Formula

Even though formulas recalculate, there may be a time when you need to actually change the formula itself. To modify an existing formula:

1. Double-click the cell that contains the formula.

2. In the Formula bar, select the existing formula and type the desired formula.

ACTIVITY 3-1

Summing a Range of Data

Objective:

Sum a range of data by using cell references.

Data Files:

- Calculations

Setup:

No files are open.

Scenario:

You have a worksheet with lots of data in it. As raw numbers, the data isn't as useful as you need it to be. One of the items you need to identify from the data is the year-to-date sales total (January through April) for Employee 123456789. After you get the year-to-date total, you decide you would also like a first quarter total for that same employee. Your first task is to create formulas that sum the range of data that make up your year-to-date and quarter totals and display them.

LESSON 3

What You Do	How You Do It

1. In the C:\My Documents\My Workbooks\Calculations file, in cell G7, **enter a formula that sums the sales results for January through April for Employee ID 123456789.**

   a. On the Standard toolbar, **click the Open button** . The Open dialog box is displayed.

   b. From the My Documents folder, **open the My Workbooks folder and select Calculations and click Open.**

   c. **Select cell G7.**

   d. **Type** *=c7+d7+e7+f7*.

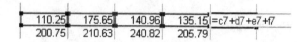

110.25	175.65	140.96	135.15	=c7+d7+e7+f7
200.75	210.63	240.82	205.79	

   As you enter each cell reference, Excel color codes each cell reference in the formula and its corresponding cell. In addition, the formula appears in the cell and in the Formula bar.

   e. On the Formula bar, **click the Enter button** to enter the formula in cell G7.

2. **What is the sales total of January through April for Employee 123456789?**

3. **Change the January sales total for Employee ID 123456789 to 123.75.**

   a. **Select cell C7.**

   b. **Type** *123.75* **and press [Enter].** Excel recalculates the result of the formula in cell G7 to reflect this change. The new total is 575.51.

4. In cell H7, **enter a formula that sums the first quarter sales for Employee ID 123456789.**

   a. **Select cell H7.**

   b. **Type** *=g7-f7* **and press [Enter].** The result is 440.36.

ACTIVITY 3-2

Completing the Formulas

Scenario:

Now, you want to enter the remaining Qtr. Totals and Tri-Totals for each employee in the Northeastern Region.

Qtr. Total	Tri-Total
575.51	440.36
857.99	652.2
901.04	590.6
851.33	601.18

Figure 3-1: *The completed formulas.*

What You Do	How You Do It
1. **Enter the formulas to calculate the Qtr. total and Tri-total values for the remaining employees. When you're finished, your worksheet will look like Figure 3-1.** When you're done, **save the file as My Calculations.**	a. In cell G8, **enter =c8+d8+e8+f8.**
	b. In cell H8, **enter =g8-f8.**
	c. In cell G9, **enter =c9+d9+e9+f9.**
	d. In cell H9, **enter =g9-f9.**
	e. In cell G10, **enter =c10+d10+e10+f10.**
	f. In cell H10, **enter =g10-f10.**
	g. **Save the file as My Calculations.**

TOPIC B

Use a Built-in Function

Now that you know how to enter basic addition and subtraction formulas, you probably realize that it can be a time-consuming task, especially if you need to enter a lot of them. Excel provides you with functions to assist you in performing calculations. In this topic, you will create formulas by using functions.

You've entered a few formulas and it seems fairly simple. However, it still involves a lot of keying, especially if a number of cells are included in your formula. You're probably thinking there must be an easier, quicker way to enter formulas, and you're right. You can use functions to simplify the process of entering formulas, including providing you with tips as you build the formula. How much easier could it be?

Functions

Definition

A *function* is a built-in formula. Functions start with the equal sign (=) and generally have two components:

- the *function name* or an abbreviation of that name; and
- the *arguments*, which are required data enclosed in parentheses.

Excel provides over 200 built-in formulas called functions. You can use a function by itself or in conjunction with other formulas or functions.

Example

Some example formulas are listed in the following table.

Functions	What It Does
=SUM(A4:A10)	This function instructs Excel to add all values in cells A4 through A10.
=AVERAGE(A4:A10)	This function instructs Excel to calculate the mean average of the values in cells A4 through A10.
=MIN(A4:A10)	This function instructs Excel to find the minimum value of the values in cells A4 through A10.
=MAX(A4:A10)	This function instructs Excel to find the maximum value of the values in cells A4 through A10.
=COUNT(A4:A10)	This function instructs Excel to find the number of entries in cells A4 through A10.

The AutoCalculate Feature

As you know, the status bar is located at the bottom of the workbook window and provides constant feedback on what's going on in any active workbook. One portion of the status bar, which may display Sum=0, reveals the findings of Excel's AutoCalculate feature. This feature is always operating in the background, working in conjunction with the selected range.

By default, AutoCalculate displays the sum of the values in the selected range. You can use AutoCalculate to do other things, such as calculate the average of a group of values, or count the number of entries in a selected range.

 It's important to note that the AutoCalculate feature only displays a value. It is not entered permanently into the worksheet anywhere, and when you deselect the range, the value is gone.

To change the calculation done by AutoCalculate, right-click on the status bar to access a shortcut menu containing the entries Average, Count, Count Nums, Max, Min, and Sum; select the function you would like to use; select a range of cells, and look at the status bar. Excel performs the function on the selected range.

Get Help on Function Arguments

The *function argument ToolTip* is a handy new feature that makes using functions much easier. When you begin typing a formula using a function, Excel displays information about function arguments. This helps users remember what they need to type for that function to work. It serves as a reference. The ToolTip that appears also contains links to related Help topics. You can see these links by hovering over the function part of the ToolTip and then clicking the link.

Use a Built-in Function

Procedure Reference: Enter a Function

To enter functions:

1. Select the cell you want to contain the function.

2. Enter the function into the cell by one of the following methods:

    *   Type the entire function directly into the cell.

    *   Type the function name and the left parenthesis, use the mouse to select the range(s) as the argument(s), separating multiple arguments with commas, and type the right parenthesis.

    *   Use the Insert Function button located on the Formula bar.

3. Press [Enter].

ACTIVITY 3-3

Using Built-in Functions

Setup:

My Calculations is open. If you did not complete the Completing the Formulas activity at the end of Topic 3A, open the file Formulas Complete and use it to continue on with this lesson.

Scenario:

Your worksheet is really starting to come together. You've entered a few basic formulas. However, now you need to add some more, and it could be a very time consuming task. You want to calculate the total January sales for the Northeastern Region, as well as determine the employees who had the highest sales and the lowest sales for the month. Your coworker, who has helped you before with Excel, suggests you use functions.

What You Do	How You Do It
1. Use the AutoCalculate feature to display the sum on the status bar of the January sales for the Northeastern Region.	a. Select the range C7:C10. b. In the status bar, **look at Sum=755**. If you select a range of cells containing numeric data, then you'll see Sum= the total of the numbers currently selected. The AutoCalculate feature allows you to perform different types of calculations using functions by selecting a range of cells in a worksheet.

2. Using the SUM function, **enter a formula in cell C12 that sums the January sales for the Northeastern Region.**

a. **Select cell C12.** You're going to enter a formula by using the SUM function.

 You can place the mouse pointer over SUM in the ToolTip to display a link and click on the link to display Microsoft Excel Help, which provides you with additional information about the SUM function.

b. **Type** *=sum(* to begin entering the formula.

Notice that as soon as Excel recognizes the function, a Function Argument ToolTip is displayed.

=sum(
SUM(**number1**, [number2], ...)

The ToolTip shows you what information you need to provide to complete this function.

c. Using the mouse, **select the range C7:C10.** As you select the range, Excel indicates how many rows and columns you're selecting.

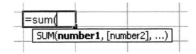

123.75	175.65	140.96
200.75	210.63	240.82
210.35	185.11	195.14
22?.15	195.37	185.66

4R x 1C
=sum(C7:C10
SUM(**number1**, [number2], ...)

The range you select appears with a flashing blue marquee around it.

d. **Type** *)* **and press [Enter]** to complete the formula. Excel calculates the sum of cells C7:C10 and places the total in cell C12, which is 755.

Let's create another formula using a different function.

3. Using the MAX function, **enter a for-mula in cell C14 that calculates the maximum sales figure for January for the Northeastern Region.**

a. **Select cell C14.**

b. **Type** *=max(.*

c. **Select the range C7:C10.**

123.75	175.65	140.96
200.75	210.63	240.82
210.35	185.11	195.14
220.15	195.37	185.66
755		

=max(C7:C10

MAX(**number1**, [number2], ...)

d. **Press [Enter].** The result is 220.15.

Notice that you didn't need to add the closing parenthesis. Excel did it for you.

4. Using the MIN function, **enter a for-mula in cell C16 that calculates the minimum sales figure for January for the Northeastern Region.**

a. **Select cell C16.**

b. **Type** *=min(.*

c. **Select the range C7:C10.**

d. **Enter the formula.** The result is 123.75.

PRACTICE ACTIVITY 3-4

Completing the Calculations

Activity Time:

15 minutes

Scenario:

You've entered the formulas using functions to make the calculations you need on the January sales numbers. Now, you need to calculate the same values for the February, March, and April sales numbers. When you're done entering your functions, your worksheet values should match those in Figure 3-2.

Employee ID	January	February	March	April
123456789	123.75	175.65	140.96	135.15
234567890	200.75	210.63	240.82	205.79
345678901	210.35	185.11	195.14	310.44
456789012	220.15	195.37	185.66	250.15
Totals	755	766.76	762.58	901.53
High	220.15	210.63	240.82	310.44
Low	123.75	175.65	140.96	135.15

Figure 3-2: *The completed functions.*

1. For the Northeastern Region, use functions to **calculate the Totals, High, and Low for February, March, and April.**

2. **Save the file.**

TOPIC C

Copy a Formula

You've created formulas in your worksheets and decide, just like your data values, you would like to re-use some of the formulas you created in other areas of your worksheet without retyping. The process for copying formulas is the same as copying data. In this topic, you will copy formulas by using the fill handle.

You've just created a number of formulas. Your brain hurts and your hands hurt from keying in all the data. There must be an easier way to enter all of the formulas, especially since so many of them are similar. You're right—there is an easier way. You can copy formulas just like you can copy text in a worksheet. By copying formulas, you'll save valuable time, and your formulas will contain fewer errors, because you aren't manually keying the formulas.

Copy a Formula

Procedure Reference: Copy a Formula Using the AutoFill Feature

In addition to copying text in a worksheet, you can also copy formulas by using the fill handle. To copy a formula using the AutoFill feature:

1. Select the cell that contains the formula you want to copy.

2. Place the mouse pointer on the fill handle.

3. When the mouse pointer changes to a + (plus sign), drag to select the cells you want to copy the formula to.

Excel adjusts copied formulas so that the cell references change relative to their new locations. These adjusting references are known as *relative references*. Keep in mind that constant values (numbers and text) are just that—constant. They don't change when you copy them to another location.

Copying to Non-adjacent Cells

The AutoFill feature is great for copying formulas in cells that are adjacent. However, what do you do if you want to copy formulas to non-adjacent cells? You can copy formulas to a nonadjacent location by using either the Copy and Paste buttons or commands, or the [Ctrl] drag method.

ACTIVITY 3-5

Copying Formulas

Objective:

Copy formulas by using the fill handle.

Setup:

My Calculations is open. If you did not complete the "Completing the Calculations" activity at the end of Topic 3B, open the file, Functions Complete, and use it to continue on with this lesson.

Scenario:

You've entered a number of formulas that include functions. However, you still have a lot more to enter. You're running out of time, and you're losing your patience. Then, you realize that you can re-use formulas by copying them. You've already created the totals, highs, and lows for January through April. So, you decide to copy those formulas for the quarter and tri-totals.

What You Do	How You Do It
1. Using the fill handle, **copy the formula for the April Total for the Northeastern Region to the Qtr. Total and Tri-total for the Northeastern Region.**	a. **Select cell F12.** You're going to copy the formula in this cell to the adjacent cells in the row.
	b. **Place the mouse pointer on the fill handle.**
	c. With the mouse pointer on the fill handle, **drag to select the range G12:H12** to copy the formula.

2. **Review the contents of cells G12 and H12.**

   Did Excel change the cell addresses relative to their new positions?

3. Use the fill handle to **copy the formulas for the April high and April low sales numbers for the Northeastern Region to calculate the Qtr. Total High and Tri-total High for the Northeastern Region. Save the file.**

a. **Select cell F14.**

b. **Place the mouse pointer on the fill handle.**

c. With the mouse pointer on the fill handle, **drag to select the range G14:H14** to copy the formula.

d. **Use the fill handle to copy the contents of cell F16 to G16:H16.**

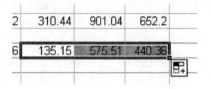

e. **Click the Save button.**

TOPIC D

Create an Absolute Reference

You've seen that Excel automatically adjusts cell references in formulas during the copy procedure to make sure that the copied formulas refer to the correct locations relative to their new position in the worksheet. There are times, however, when you might not want to adjust all of the cell references, such as when a number referred to in a formula appears in only one cell. In this topic, you will copy formulas without adjusting cell references by using absolute references.

Now that you've copied some formulas, you want to copy some more. Suppose you copy a formula and you don't get the desired results. The cell references changed relative to their new locations. You didn't want that to happen. In this case, you can change the formula that you're going to copy so that the cells don't automatically update and the copied formulas display the correct values.

Absolute References

An *absolute reference* is a cell reference in a formula that doesn't change when you copy the formula. To prevent column or row references, or both, from changing when you copy a formula containing them, you must write the formula by using absolute references. To create an absolute reference, insert dollar signs ($) before the column and row designation. For instance, F22 becomes F22.

Create an Absolute Reference

Procedure Reference: Make a Cell Reference Absolute

There will be instances where you'll want to make a cell reference absolute rather than relative. To do that:

1. Double-click on the cell that contains the formula you want to contain absolute references.

2. Place the insertion point in the cell reference.

3. Press [F4], the Absolute Reference Key.

4. Enter the formula.

ACTIVITY 3-6

Creating Absolute References

Objective:

Edit a formula so that a portion of it doesn't change when you copy it.

Setup:

My Calculations is open.

Scenario:

With all this practice, you're a wiz at copying formulas. You create a formula that calculates the commission for employee 123456789. You try to copy the commission for Employee ID 123456789 to Employee ID 234567890 to save yourself some time, and you don't get the results you expected. You realize that the cell references changed relative to the formula's new location. However, you need each formula to refer to the specific cell containing the sales commission percentage. You decide you need to create absolute references before you copy.

What You Do	How You Do It
1. Create a formula that calculates the commission for Employee ID 123456789 by multiplying the Commission Rate by the Qtr. Total.	a. **Select cell I7.** You're going to enter a formula that calculates the commission earnings for the employee listed in row 7.
	b. **Type =** to start the formula. You'll complete the formula by selecting cells in the worksheet.

c. **Click on cell H3.** This cell contains the commission rate. Excel adds H3 to the formula.

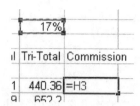

d. **Type *.** You'll multiply two values.

e. **Click on cell G7.**

This cell contains the total sales figure for the employee listed in row 7.

f. **Press [Enter]** to display the result, 97.8367, in cell I7.

2. **Copy the commission for Employee ID 123456789 to the rest of the employees in the Northeastern Region.**

    What is the result?

3. Using the Formula bar and the absolute reference key, **correct the calculation errors by creating an absolute reference for commission for Employee ID 123456789.**

    a. **Double-click on cell I7 and delete its contents.**

    b. In the Formula bar, **type the formula =G7*H3**, as shown in the following graphic.

    ✕ ✓ _fx_ =G7*H3

c. **Press [F4].** Excel inserts dollar signs in front of the H and the 3. The H3 reference is now an absolute reference, rather than a relative reference.

✕ ✓ ƒx =G7*H3

d. **Enter the formula.** The other commissions below this one still reflect the results of the previous copy.

Let's copy the formula again and see what happens.

4. **Copy the commission for Employee ID 123456789 to the rest of the employees in the Northeastern Region.**

What is the result?

5. **Save and close all open files.**

a. **Save the file(s) using the method of your choice.**

b. **Close any open files.**

Lesson 3 Follow-up

In this lesson, you worked with calculations. You took the numeric data that was already contained in a worksheet and performed calculations on it, such as addition and subtraction, by creating formulas by selecting ranges and using built-in functions. You also copied formulas and created absolute references. Now, you can be assured that your calculations are accurate and will be updated automatically if the numeric data changes.

1. **Identify some advantages of using Excel's built-in functions.**

2. **In your worksheets, what types of formulas will you create?**

NOTES

LESSON 4
Formatting

Lesson Time
55 minutes

Lesson Objectives:

In this lesson, you will change the appearance of worksheet data by using a variety of formatting techniques.

You will:

* Use the Format Cells dialog box to format cells that contain numeric data.

* Create a custom number format.

* Change the font size and type of worksheet data.

* Use the Format→Style command to apply styles to worksheet data.

* Add borders to cells.

* Find and replace cell data and formats.

* Change column width and row height.

* Align the contents of cells by using a variety of alignment options.

* Use the Merge And Center button to merge and center cells.

* Format the cells in a worksheet by using the AutoFormat feature.

Introduction

You have a worksheet complete with both text and numeric data, plus values you've calculated from your numeric data. Now, you want to enhance the appearance of that data. In this lesson, you change the appearance of worksheet data by using a variety of formatting techniques.

All your data is entered in your worksheet, along with formulas to calculate that data. You're proud of the work you've done. However, the worksheet would be more valuable if some of the more crucial data was somehow emphasized. Excel provides you with numerous options for formatting selected data in your worksheets. By using formatting, you'll be on your way to a worksheet that can be effectively displayed and interpreted.

TOPIC A

Specify Number Formats

When you're working with formatting in Excel, one of the most common formats you can apply to data is number formats. In this topic, you will specify a number format for a selected range of data.

Sometimes the data in a worksheet doesn't appear the way you want it to display. If that happens, it may not be interpreted the way you expect. For example, the number 200 may not be interpreted as succinctly as $200.00. You can easily change the format of specific data to enhance its display and ensure that it will be interpreted correctly. You can change the numeric format of a number by using a few quick steps.

Number Formats

Definition

A *number format* changes the appearance of numbers displayed in a cell without changing the actual number entered in the cell.

 This is the displayed value versus the actual value you learned about in the lesson on formulas.

Excel provides you with a variety of number formats to choose from. Table 4-1 outlines those number formats.

Table 4-1: *The Number Formats Available in Excel*

Category	Description
General	Has no specific format. Contents of the cell are displayed as you enter them.
Number	Used for a general display of numbers. By default, two decimal places are shown.
Currency	Used for general monetary values. Numbers are displayed with a dollar sign ($) and two decimal points.
Accounting	Formats the same as currency, but also lines up the currency symbols and decimal points in the column.

Category	Description
Date	Displays date and time serial numbers as date values. By default, it is displayed as mm/dd/yyyy.
Time	Displays date and time serial numbers as time values. By default, it is displayed as hr:min AM/PM.
Percentage	Multiplies the cell value by 100 and display with a percent symbol.
Fraction	Displays as a fraction.
Scientific	Displays as a scientific format.
Text	Treated as text even if a number is in the cell.
Special	Used for tracking list and database values.
Custom	Used as a starting point when creating a custom code.

Example

For example, suppose you have a cell that contains the value 75.25. When it's formatted as currency with zero decimal places, Excel displays the value $75 in your worksheet. However, the actual value used by Excel is 75.25. When you select this cell, the number displayed in the formula bar is 75.25. In addition, Excel uses the actual value, 75.25, when the cell is referenced in a formula.

Specify Number Formats

Procedure Reference: Change the Appearance of Numbers

The default number format for Excel worksheets is the General format. Typically, when you enter a number into a cell with the General format, the number appears the way that you enter it. You can use Excel's built-in formats to change the appearance of numbers.

1. Select the range of numbers to which you want to apply the format.

2. Choose Format→Cells to display the Format Cells dialog box.

3. If necessary, select the Number tab.

4. Select the desired format category.

5. If applicable, select the desired number of decimal places for the number format you selected.

 When you select a format category that allows for decimal places, you can use the default of two, or use the Decimal Places text box to change the number of decimal places to fit your needs.

6. Click OK.

The Narrow Column ToolTip

By default, Excel adjusts the width of a column to accommodate an increase in space needed when a number format is applied to a cell. However, if you have manually changed the column width, when the total number of characters for numeric data is greater than the column width, number signs (#####) appear in the cell. This is to prevent you from inadvertently using a truncated number without realizing it. For example, the number in the cell is 123456, but only 12345 will display in the cell. You don't want to see 12345 if the value is really 123456.

To display the number, you can change the formatting, enlarge the width of the column, or use the Narrow Column ToolTip. This ToolTip allows you to see the contents of cells that are displayed as number signs because the width of the column is too small to display the full value.

ACTIVITY 4-1

Specifying a Numeric Format

Objective:

Change the default numeric format of a range of cells from General to Currency or Number.

Data Files:

• Formatting

Setup:

No files are open.

Scenario:

Your boss takes a look at all the editing changes you've made to the worksheet and is very pleased. However, he wants to enhance the worksheet by having you make some formatting changes to it. The first change he wants you to make is to apply the Number format to all of the numeric data in the worksheet (except the dates) and the Currency format to the commissions.

What You Do	How You Do It
1. In the Formatting file, change the number format of the range C7:I10 to Number.	a. Open the file, Formatting.
	b. Select the range C7:I10.
	c. Choose Format→Cells to display the Format Cells dialog box. You can use this dialog box to change the number, alignment, font, border, and pattern of cells.

d. On the Number tab, **select Number and verify that the setting for Decimal Places is 2.**

Click OK to close the Format Cells dialog box and apply the formatting.

---

2. **How are the formatted numbers displayed?**

---

3. **Change the numeric format of the range C12:H16 to Currency and observe the display of the numbers.**

   a. **Select cells C12:H16.**

   b. **Choose Format→Cells.**

   c. From the Category list box, **select Currency.**

   d. **Click OK.** Excel displays all numbers in the Currency format with two decimal places. All of the columns have been widened automatically to display the additional formatting characters, except column H. Excel displays number signs (#####) in cell H12, which indicates that the number is too large to fit in the column.

---

4. **What happens when you place the mouse pointer over cell H12?**

We'll fix the column width later in this lesson.

5. Apply the Currency format to cells K7:O10 and save the file as *My Formatting*.

 a. Select cells K7:O10.

 b. Using the Format Cell dialog box, **apply the Currency format**.

 c. Save the file as C:\My Documents\My Formatting.

TOPIC B

Create a Custom Number Format

Once you know how to apply a numeric format to data, you might want to create your own number format. In this topic, you will create a custom number format.

Suppose you have a range of numeric data that you want to format so it's easier to read. The Employee IDs are actually employee social security numbers, but it's hard to know that without any formatting. However, Excel doesn't provide the exact format that you want for that data. By using the Custom format category, you can create your own formats. Creating your own formats makes it easier to enter numeric data that's specific to your unique applications.

Create a Custom Number Format

Procedure Reference: Create a Custom Format

One of the number formats that Excel provides is Custom. You can use one of the custom formats as a starting point for creating your own number format. To create a custom format:

1. Display the Format Cells dialog box.

2. From the Category list box, select Custom.

3. From the Type list, select the appropriate type.

4. Using the Type text box, add or remove formatting codes as needed.

5. Click OK.

ACTIVITY 4-2

Creating and Applying a Custom Format

Objective:

Create and apply a custom number format, building on the social security number format.

Setup:

My Formatting is open.

Scenario:

You have a range of data that includes Employee IDs. You want to format the data, but none of the number format categories that Excel provides are appropriate. You decide to create your own custom number format based on the Excel social security style number format. You want to add the text *SS* before the sequence of numbers.

What You Do	How You Do It
1. **Identify the Excel custom number format you should base your custom social security format on.**	a. **Select the cells B7:B10.** b. **Display the Format Cells dialog box for all Employee IDs for the Northeastern Region.** c. **Select the Custom category.**

2. **What format type will display the numbers like a social security number?**

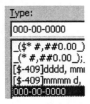

3. **Using the Type text box, edit the selected type to display as "SS" 000-00-0000 and apply the custom format.** **Save the file.**	a. **In the Type text box, click to place the insertion point before the first 0.**

b. **Type "SS". Press [spacebar]** to include a space before the social security number.

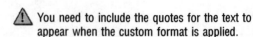

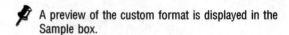

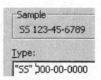 You need to include the quotes for the text to appear when the custom format is applied.

📌 A preview of the custom format is displayed in the Sample box.

c. **Click OK** to apply the custom format to the selected range of cells.

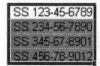

d. **Save the file by using the same name.**

TOPIC C

Change Font Size and Type

Now, you know how to apply some basic formatting in Excel, including applying bold, italic, and underline attributes, plus number formats to data. Another change you can make to your data is altering the font size and type. In this topic, you will change the font size and type of selected data.

Did you ever look at a document and notice that the text or numbers were difficult to read? Maybe the font size was too small, the typeface was too busy, or critical information was not clearly identified? By changing the font size or type, you can change the appearance of your data in Excel to make it easier to read and find critical data.

Fonts

A *font* is the typeface and size of a set of characters. Typeface is a design for a set of characters, such as Times New Roman. Size is measured in points. In Excel the default font is 10 point, Arial. Suppose you want to change it to Times New Roman, 12 point. You can change the font for the whole worksheet or for selected cells.

Change Font Size and Type

Procedure Reference: Change the Font

To change the font:

1. Select the cells you want to format.

2. On the Formatting toolbar, from the Font drop-down list, select a font.

3. On the Formatting toolbar, from the Font Size drop-down list, select a font size.

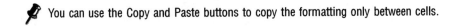 You can use the Copy and Paste buttons to copy the formatting only between cells.

ACTIVITY 4-3

Changing Font Size and Type

Setup:

My Formatting is open.

Scenario:

You've already applied bold formatting to some of the text in your worksheet to make it stand out. However, the titles and headings still aren't making the visual impact you would like. You decide to change the font size and type of the titles for the Northeastern Region and Mideastern Region to Book Antiqua, 18 point.

What You Do	How You Do It
1. Using the Font drop-down list, change the font type of the Northeastern Region title to Book Antiqua.	a. Select cell A1.

b. On the Formatting toolbar, **click on the drop-down arrow beside the Font text box.** Excel displays a list of available fonts.

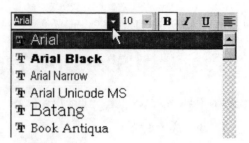

c. **Select Book Antiqua.** Excel applies the Book Antiqua font to the text in cell A1. The Font text box displays the selected font.

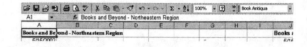

2. **Change the font size for the North-eastern Region title to 18.**

a. **Click on the drop-down arrow beside the Font Size text box.** Excel displays a list of available font sizes.

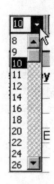

b. **Select 18** to increase the size of the text. Excel displays the selected font size in the Font Size text box.

3. **Change the font size and type of the Mideastern Region title to 18 point, Book Antiqua, bold. When you're done, save the file.**

    a. **Select cell J1.**

    b. From the Font drop-down list, **select Book Antiqua.**

    c. From the Font Size drop-down list, **select 18.**

    d. **Save the file by using the same name.**

TOPIC D

Apply Styles

You've learned how to apply individual formatting options to your data. Now you're going to learn how to apply a group of individual formats, called a style, to a particular set of data.

Suppose you have a series of data that is repeated throughout your worksheet. In addition, one of those data series has some formatting applied to it that you want to apply to the other data. You can create a style that includes all those individual format options and then apply that style to all the other similar data. For example, suppose you have a list of months, January through June, in three locations in a worksheet. You want them all to be formatted with bold and italic. Instead of selecting all three ranges and applying the bold format, then the italic format, you can apply a single style to all three ranges that includes both desired attributes. Styles will save you time and ensure that your worksheet data is consistent where necessary.

Styles

A *style* is a collection of individual format options that you can apply at the same time to selected cells. Each style can include the following elements:

- Number
- Alignment
- Font
- Border
- Patterns
- Protection

For example, by default, the Normal style is applied to all cells in a new worksheet. That style includes the General number format, Bottom Alignment, 10 point size, Arial typeface, no borders or shading, and the protection is locked.

Apply Styles

Procedure Reference: Create a Style

To create a style:

1. Apply the formatting you want in your style to a cell.

2. Verify that the cell is selected and choose Format→Style.

3. In the Style Name text box, type a name for your style.

4. Click Add.

5. Click Close.

Procedure Reference: Apply a Style

To apply a style:

1. Select the cells you want to format.

2. Choose Format→Style to display the Style dialog box.

3. Select a style from the Style Name drop-down list.

4. Click OK.

ACTIVITY 4-4

Creating and Applying a Style

Setup:

My Formatting is open.

Scenario:

You have applied a custom number format to the Employee IDs for the Northeastern Region. You decide that data would look better if it was also italic. You know that you'll be applying both these format options to other Employee IDs that you enter, so you decide to create a style to include both your custom number format and the italic attribute. Once you've created the style, you use it to format the Employee IDs for the Mideastern Region.

What You Do	How You Do It
1. Apply the italic attribute to the Employee IDs for the Northeastern Region.	a. Select cells B7:B10.
	b. Click the Italic button.

2. **Create a style, called My Style, based on the formatting of cells B7:B10.**

    a. **Choose Format→Style** to display the Style dialog box.

    b. In the Style Name text box, **type My Style.**

    c. **Click Add** to define the style without applying it to the selected cells.

    d. **Click Close** to close the Style dialog box.

3. **What elements does the style include?**

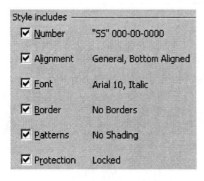

4. **Apply the style, My Style, to the Employee IDs for the Mideastern Region and observe the results.**

    a. **Select cells K7:K10.**

    b. **Choose Format→Style** to display the Style dialog box.

    c. From the Style Name drop-down list, **select My Style.**

    d. **Click OK.**

    e. **Look at the selected cells.** The style you indicated has been applied, including the custom number format and italic attribute.

TOPIC E

Add Borders and Color to Cells

You might be thinking that you've probably applied most of the formatting options available in Excel. Not exactly–there are still quite a few others. One of those other options is borders. In this topic, you will add borders to selected cells.

Okay, so the formats you've applied so far to your worksheet aren't knocking you off your feet yet. You need to apply a format that will really make specific cells stand out. You decide to use borders, because you feel they will really bring the level of emphasis that you need to those cells.

Add Borders and Color to Cells

Procedure Reference: Apply Borders or Colors

To emphasize data, you can add border lines or color to cells. A variety of border types, widths, and colors are available in Excel. To apply borders or colors:

1. Select the cells that you want to format.

2. Click on the drop-down arrow next to the Borders or Fill Color buttons on the Formatting toolbar.

3. Select an option from the palette.

 You can use the Borders toolbar to draw and erase borders and change the line style and color of borders.

ACTIVITY 4-5

Adding Borders and Color to Cells

Objective:

Apply borders and colors to selected cells.

Setup:

My Formatting is open.

Scenario:

Your boss has requested that specific cells in the worksheet be emphasized more than others. You know that some of the common formatting options, such as bold and italic, won't achieve the result he wants. For the Northeastern Region, you decide to apply a thick box border and turquoise fill color to the Commission Rate heading and a bottom border under the headings for the region.

What You Do	How You Do It
1. Apply a thick box border to the commission rate for the Northeastern Region and view the newly formatted cell.	a. **Select cell H3.** b. On the Formatting toolbar, **click the drop-down arrow beside the Borders button** ⬚. A border palette is displayed from which you can choose a border style. c. **Select Thick Box Border.**

Thick Box Border

d. **Click on any other cell** to deselect cell H3.

e. **Look at the emphasis that the border places on cell H3.**

2. **Apply the fill color Turquoise to the commission rate heading for the Northeastern Region and view the formatting.**

   a. **Select cell H3.**

   b. On the Formatting toolbar, **click on the drop-down arrow beside the Fill Color button** 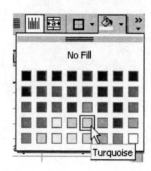. A color palette is displayed.

   c. Using ScreenTips to identify the colors, **select Turquoise.**

   d. **Click on any other cell** to deselect cell H3.

   e. **View the formatting.** Now, let's draw some borders.

3. **Draw a bottom border under the data headings for the Northeastern Region.**

   a. **Click on the drop-down arrow beside the Borders button and click on Draw Borders.** The Borders toolbar is displayed.

    Notice that the mouse pointer has changed to a pencil.

   b. **Click on the bottom border of cell B5 and drag across to cell I5.**

Employee ID	January	February	March	April	Qtr. Total	Tri-Total	Commission

   c. On the Borders toolbar, **click the Draw Borders button** to turn off the Draw Borders feature.

PRACTICE ACTIVITY 4-6

Applying Additional Borders and Fill Colors

Activity Time:

10 minutes

Scenario:

Now that you know how to apply borders and fill colors to cells, you can apply the same formatting to the mideastern region's commission rate and headings in the worksheet.

				Commission Rate:	17%		
Employee ID	January	February	March	April	Qtr. Total	Tri-Total	Commission

Figure 4-1: *The completed borders and colors.*

1. Apply the Thick Box Border and the fill color Turquoise to cell Q3.

2. Apply a bottom border to cells K5:R5 using the method of your choice.

3. Compare your results to those in Figure 4-1.

TOPIC F

Find and Replace Formats

At this point, you have all your data in your worksheet and you've applied formatting to both text and numeric data. What if you realize that you need to change a specific format that appears throughout the worksheet? You've used the Find And Replace command to search for numeric data. You can use it to search for formatting, too. In this topic, you will use the Find and Replace command to find and replace cell formatting.

Suppose you have a worksheet that contains the same data repeatedly throughout the worksheet. You realize that the format you've applied to the data is incorrect. You need to replace the formatting of all instances. The Find and Replace feature can save you time by finding and replacing cell formats. By using the Find and Replace feature, you can be assured that you won't miss any instances, as you might if you tried to make the changes manually.

Find and Replace Formats

Procedure Reference: Find and Replace Cell Formats

To find and replace cell formats:

1. Click on any cell in the worksheet to search the entire worksheet. To search a specific range of cells, select that range only.

2. Choose Edit→Replace to display the Find And Replace dialog box.

3. You can do one of the following for both the Find What and Replace With options:

   To specify a format:
   A. Click Options.
   B. Click Format.
   C. Set your options in the Find Format dialog box.

   To use a specific cell format as an example:
   A. Click Format.
   B. Choose Choose Format From Cell.
   C. Select the example cell from your worksheet.

4. Click Find Next.

5. To replace the selected occurrence of formatting, click Replace. To replace all occurrences of formatting, click Replace All.

6. When you're done with the search, click Close.

ACTIVITY 4-7

Finding and Replacing Formats

Setup:

My Formatting is open. If you did not complete the practice activity that appears after Activity 4-5, open the Formatting Complete file and use it to continue with this lesson.

Scenario:

Another formatting change that your boss wants you to make is to the custom format of the employee IDs. He wants to change the display of the custom format from *SS 000-00-000* to *SS # 000-00-000*. You believe this change is going to take some time, because you'll have to change all the effected cells manually or use copy and paste. You don't want to miss any cells. Your coworker suggests you use the Find and Replace command to quickly and accurately make the formatting changes.

What You Do	How You Do It
1. **Display the Find And Replace dialog box and set the Find What text box to include the format from cell B7.**	a. **Choose Edit→Replace** to display the Find And Replace dialog box. b. **Click Options.** c. **Display the Find What Format shortcut menu.** 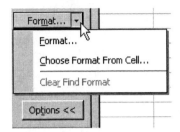 **Choose Choose Format From Cell.** The mouse pointer changes to a dropper with a cross. The Find And Replace dialog box is temporarily hidden. d. **Click on cell B7.** The Find And Replace dialog box is redisplayed. The format of cell B7 has been placed in the Find What Format box. 
2. **Set the Replace With text box to include the custom numeric format SS # 000-00-0000.**	a. **Click the Replace With Format button.**  The Replace Format dialog box is displayed. b. **Select the Custom Category.** c. **Select the "SS" 000-00-0000 type.** d. **Change the Type to read "SS #" 000-00-0000.** e. **Click OK.**

3. With cell A1 active, **use the Find And Replace dialog box to find and replace all instances of the selected formats.**

a. **Click outside the Find And Replace dialog box** to access the worksheet window.

b. **Press [Ctrl][Home]** to return to cell A1.

c. **Click Find Next.** Cell B7 is active.

d. **Click Replace.** Excel replaces the contents of cell B7 with number signs (#####) indicating that the contents of the cell are too large to be displayed in the column.

e. **Use the Narrow Column ToolTip to display the contents of cell B7.**

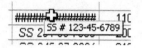

✏ We'll fix the number signs (#####) in the next topic.

f. **Click Replace All** to replace the remaining instances of formatting. A message box is displayed indicating the number of replacements. There were 7.

g. **Click OK** to clear the message box.

h. **Click Close.**

TOPIC G

Change Column Width and Row Height

The Find and Replace feature is a very useful tool. However, as you've seen from the previous exercise, when you're finding and replacing data, you might end up with columns or rows that are not wide enough for the data within them. In this topic, you will change column width and row height.

Let's say you have a worksheet that contains some very important data. However, some of the cell contents are displayed with number signs (#####) because their corresponding columns are not wide enough to display the data. By widening those columns, your data will display as you intended it to. In addition, some of the data in the rows seems cramped. It would look much better if you could increase the row height.

Change Column Width and Row Height

Procedure Reference: Change the Width of Worksheet Columns Manually

Once you apply formatting to an entire worksheet, a column might not be wide enough for the contents of some of the cells. If the number in the active cell is too wide for the column, the column width adjusts automatically so that the number appears. You can also change the width of worksheet columns manually.

1. To change the column width, you can do any of the following:
   - Place the mouse pointer on the boundary to the right of a column heading, and drag the divider to the right (to expand the column) or to the left (to shrink the column).
   - Place the mouse pointer on the boundary to the right of a column heading and double-click the mouse button. Excel calculates the column width to accommodate the longest entry in the column.
   - Select a cell in one or more columns, choose Format→Column→Width, type the new width, and click OK.

Procedure Reference: Change the Row Height

You might find after changing the text in a row that the height of the row needs to be changed. For example, maybe you rotated some text in a row and now that text seems a bit crunched. Like changing column width, Excel provides you with a number of ways to change the row height, including the following:

1. To change the row height, you can do any of the following:
   - Place the mouse pointer on the boundary of the appropriate row heading, and drag the divider up or down as needed.
   - Place the mouse pointer on the boundary on the appropriate row heading and double-click the mouse button. Excel calculates the row height to accommodate the highest entry in the column.
   - Select a cell in one or more rows, choose Format→Row→Height, type the new height, and click OK.

To change the row height of multiple rows, select the rows you want to change, and drag a boundary below a selected row heading.

ACTIVITY 4-8

Changing Column Width and Row Height in Your Worksheet

Setup:
My Formatting is open.

Scenario:
You have a worksheet that's displaying a series of number signs (#####) in the Employee ID columns and you need to get the true cell values to display. Specifically, you want to increase the width of the Employee ID column for the Northeastern Region to 15.29 and have Excel autocalculate the column widths for the Northeastern Region Tri-total and Employee ID columns. You also want the row height of the headings to be increased to 19.5. You decide to change the column widths and row heights.

What You Do	How You Do It
1. Change the width of Employee ID column for the Northeastern Region to 15.29.	a. In the column heading, **point to the boundary between the headings for columns B and C.** A double-headed arrow is displayed.
To change the column width of multiple columns, select the columns you want to change, and drag a boundary to the right of a selected column heading.	b. **Drag the boundary to the right until the ScreenTip displays 15.29.**
	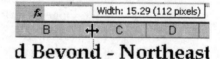
	Now, all the contents of column B are displayed. Let's fix column H.
2. Change the width of column H until the Tri-total for the Northeastern Region is displayed.	a. **Double-click on the boundary between the headings for columns H and I.** Column H is automatically sized to fit the widest data in the column.
3. Change the width of column K until all of the Employee IDs are displayed.	a. **Double-click on the boundary between the headings for columns K and L.**

4.   **Change the height of row 5 to 19.50.**

a.   In the row heading, **point to the boundary between the headings for rows 5 and 6.**

b.   **Drag the boundary down until the ScreenTip displays 19.50.**

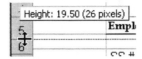

Now, there's a bit more room for the titles.

c.   **Save the file by using the same name.**

TOPIC H

Align Cell Contents

An additional formatting change that you might want to make is to change the alignment of the data within a cell. In this topic, you will align the contents of cells.

Have you ever looked at a printed copy of a document or worksheet and noticed that the alignment of some of the data doesn't look correct? For example, you have a heading for a column of data that doesn't line up with the data underneath. The heading title looks lost above the data. With the alignment options in Excel, you can align cell contents so that the heading is displayed effectively.

Align Cell Contents

Procedure Reference: Align the Contents of a Cell

You can change the alignment of text or numbers in a cell. Right-aligned, left-aligned, and centered are the most common alignments. To align the contents of a cell:

1.   Select the cell.

2.   Click the desired alignment button on the Formatting toolbar.

ACTIVITY 4-9

Aligning Cell Contents

Setup:

My Formatting is open.

Scenario:

Now that you've changed the height of the row containing your heading for the Northeastern Region, you decide that you're still not satisfied with the way the heading for that row is displaying relative to the data. So, you decide to center the headings.

What You Do	How You Do It
1. Change the alignment of the headings for the Northeastern Region to center and observe the results.	a. **Select the range B5:I5.** You're going to right-align the contents of the selected cells.
	b. On the Formatting toolbar, **click the Center button**.
	c. **Look at the selected cells.**

The data looks better. However, column I is too small to display all of the text in cell I5.

d. **Change the width of the Commission column for the Northeastern Region to fit the widest text in the column.**

2. Change the alignment of the headings for the Mideastern Region to center and save the file.

a. Select the range K5:R5.

b. On the Formatting toolbar, **click the Center button.**

Like column I, column R is too small to display all of the text in cell R5.

c. **Change the width of the Commission column for the Mideastern Region to fit the widest text in the column.**

d. **Save the file by using the same name.**

TOPIC I

Merge and Center Cells

Now that you've centered data within a single cell, another alignment option that you might want to apply to your data is to center text across a range. In this topic, you will merge and split cells.

The actual data for the titles of your worksheet is contained in one cell, but the text is so long that it spreads across a number of cells. Any alignment change you make applies to the single cell and not the range your title spills over into. The title looks terrible because it isn't centered across the cells in which it is displayed. You can use the Merge And Center button to center text across a range of cells, enhancing the appearance of your worksheet.

Merge and Center Cells

Procedure Reference: Center Text Across a Range of Cells

You might want to center text across a range of cells; for example, a heading for a group of numbers. To do so:

1. Select the range to center across.

2. Click the Merge And Center button.

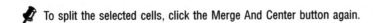 To split the selected cells, click the Merge And Center button again.

Storage of Cell Contents

Even though Excel centers the title across the range, Excel stores the text in only one cell. Remember, the Formula bar always shows the true contents of a cell, while the worksheet display might be different.

Using the Go To Command

When you're making changes to a worksheet, you might find it handy to use the Go To command. Simply press [F5] or choose Edit→Go To, and in the Go To dialog box, enter the appropriate cell reference and click OK.

ACTIVITY 4-10

Merging and Centering Cells

Setup:

My Formatting is open.

Scenario:

Suppose you've finished all the formatting that your boss has requested. However, as you look at the completed worksheet, one thing is bothering you. The titles of each section of data are displaying across a range of cells, but they aren't centered within the range of cells. You decide to center the titles of each section across the group of cells where the title is displayed.

What You Do	How You Do It
1. **Return to the beginning of the worksheet by using the Go To feature.**	a. **Press [F5]** to display the Go To dialog box.
	b. In the Reference text box, **type *a1*.**
	c. **Click OK.** The active cell is now A1.
2. **Using the Merge And Center button, center the Northeastern Region title.**	a. **Select cells A1:G1.**
	b. On the Formatting toolbar, **click the Merge And Center button** .
	c. **Look at the text.** The title text in cell A1 is centered across the selected range.
3. **Using the Merge And Center button, center the Mideastern Region title.**	a. **Select cells J1:O1.**
	b. **Click the Merge And Center button.**

4. Using the Merge And Center button, center the Commission Rate text for the Northeastern Region.	a. **Select cells F3:G3.** b. **Click the Merge And Center button.** You decide you don't like this change.
5. Using the Merge And Center button, split the Commission Rate text for the Northeastern Region.	a. **Verify that cell F3 is selected.** b. **Click the Merge And Center button.** The text is again split across the selected cells. c. **Save the file using the same name.**

TOPIC J

Apply an AutoFormat

Now that you've made all these formatting changes to your worksheet, you might be wondering if there's an easier way to format your worksheet. There is. In this topic, you will use the AutoFormat feature.

Have you ever had a worksheet or document that you wanted to format quickly? Suppose you wanted all the heading text to include borders and all the numeric data to be colored, but you didn't know how to, or the only way you knew how was to make each formatting change individually. Well, Excel provides you with the AutoFormat feature that allows you to quickly change the format of selected cells, saving you time and making your worksheet look great too.

AutoFormat

AutoFormat is a built-in group of cell formats that you can apply to a range of data. AutoFormats can include such formatting options as font size, patterns, and alignment. For example, suppose you wanted to apply the AutoFormat Simple to a selected range. That AutoFormat would include some bolded text and borders.

Apply an AutoFormat

Procedure Reference: Apply an AutoFormat

If you don't want to apply formats individually to selected cells or if you just want to save time, you can use the AutoFormat feature. With AutoFormat, you can quickly change the format of selected cells by choosing from a variety of predefined formats that Excel provides for you.

To apply an AutoFormat:

1. Select the cells that you want to format.

2. Choose Format→AutoFormat to display the AutoFormat dialog box.

3. Select the format of your choice.

4. Click OK.

ACTIVITY 4-11

Applying an AutoFormat

Setup:

My Formatting is open.

Scenario:

You can let out a big sigh of relief. You're finished with all of those changes your boss requested. However, now that you know how to do all this formatting, your friendly co-worker gives you a little tip. You can easily format a selected range of cells by using the AutoFormat feature. You tell your co-worker thanks for the tip (better late than never). Lucky for you, though, that your co-worker clued you in, because your boss just handed you the worksheet, and he wants you to quickly change the formatting of the worksheet so that each region's data is more professional looking. You decide to use the List 2 AutoFormat.

What You Do	How You Do It
1. Apply the List 2 AutoFormat to the column headings and each row of data for each employee in the Northeastern Region and fix any column sizing issues that arise due to the formatting.	a. Select cells B5:I10.
	b. Choose Format→AutoFormat to display the AutoFormat dialog box. You can use this dialog box to select a predefined format for a selected range of cells.
	c. Scroll down and select the List 2 autoformat.

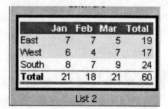

d. **Click OK** to close the dialog box and apply the AutoFormat.

Employee ID	January	February	March	April	Qtr. Total	Tri-Total	Commission
SS # 123-45-6789	110.25	175.65	140.96	135.15	562.01	426.86	95.54
SS # 234-56-7890	200.75	210.63	240.82	205.79	857.99	652.20	145.86
SS # 345-67-8901	210.35	185.11	195.14	310.44	901.04	590.60	153.18
SS # 456-78-9012	220.15	195.37	185.66	250.15	851.33	601.18	144.73

e. **Widen the Tri-Total column for the Northeastern Region** to display the contents of all cells.

2. **Apply the AutoFormat of your choice to the column headings and each row of data for each employee in the Mideastern Region.**

   a. **Select cells K5:R10.**

   b. **Choose Format→AutoFormat.**

   c. **Select the autoformat of your choice.**

   d. **Click OK.**

3. **Save and close all files.**

   a. **Save the files by using the same name.**

   b. **Close all files.**

Lesson 4 Follow-up

In this lesson, you applied formatting to your worksheet. Some of those formats include applying number formats to numeric data, changing the font size and type, adding borders and colors to cells, changing the column width and row height, and applying an AutoFormat. You can now take the formatting skills you learned in this lesson and apply them to your worksheets, enhancing their appearance and making the data interpreted more easily.

1. **What types of formatting will you apply to your worksheets?**

2. **Will you apply formats individually to your worksheets, or will you use the AutoFormat feature? Why?**

NOTES

LESSON 5
Working with Multiple Worksheets

Lesson Time
40 minutes

Lesson Objectives:

In this lesson, you will work with multiple worksheets by formatting, repositioning, copying and moving, and adding and deleting worksheets within a workbook.

You will:

* Format the worksheet tabs.
* Move worksheet tabs.
* Copy worksheets.
* Add and delete worksheets.

LESSON 5

Introduction

You have already learned the basics of getting started in Excel, how to perform calculations and format single worksheets. Now, you will work with multiple worksheets. You will format your worksheet tabs, move, copy, insert, and delete worksheets.

Most Excel workbooks have multiple worksheets. Knowing how to format, move, copy, insert, and delete worksheets is a necessity if you are going to be an effective Excel user. You may not use multiple worksheets in your workbook, but if you are sent a workbook with multiple worksheets by a co-worker, or your boss, you will want to know how to work with them.

TOPIC A

Format Worksheet Tabs

Now that you have created and modified your worksheet, you may have noticed that there are, and can be, multiple worksheets in a workbook. One way to organize these worksheets is by formatting the worksheet tabs. You will name the worksheet tabs and then you will change the color of the tabs.

Changing the name and color of the worksheet tabs allows you to further organize your workbook. For example, if you had a workbook that contained information on the different departments in your company, you could change the color of the worksheet tab that represents each department's data. Adding names to worksheet tabs allows you to easily identify the contents of each worksheet and makes navigation in a multi-sheet workbook much easier.

Format Worksheet Tabs

By now you know that the default Excel workbook contains three worksheets named Sheet1, Sheet2, and Sheet3. A worksheet's name appears on its sheet tab. When the sheet is active, the name appears in bold on its sheet tab.

Procedure Reference: Format Your Worksheet Tab

You can change the color of the worksheet tab as a way of applying formatting to the worksheet tab in order to make it easier to distinguish between tabs. To format your worksheet tab:

1. To change the color of the worksheet tab:
    A. Right-click on the worksheet tab.
    B. Choose Tab Color.
    C. Select the color of your choice.
    D. Click OK.

2. To change the title of a worksheet tab:
    A. Right-click on the worksheet tab.
    B. Choose Rename.

> You can also double-click on the worksheet tab to put it in Edit mode and change the title of the tab.

C.   Type the new name of the sheet tab.

D.   Press [Enter].

ACTIVITY 5-1

Format Your Worksheet Tabs

Data Files:

- Multisheet Workbook

Setup:

No files are open.

Scenario:

Your manager has just given you the task of keeping the department information (which is contained in an Excel worksheet) organized and updated. The worksheet consists of four different divisions in your department as well as a summary page. The data for each division is contained on separate worksheets. One way that you would like to organize the worksheet is to color code it, adding color to each area for easy identification. You would also like to rename the sheet tabs so that it is easy to identify which sheet contains what information. You will start by renaming the worksheets based on the worksheet title and then you will add different colors to the worksheet tabs. When you are finished, your workbook should look like Figure 5-1.

| Australian Division | European Division | N American Division | S American Division | **Summary** |

Figure 5-1: *Multisheet Workbook after the activity has been completed.*

What You Do	How You Do It
1. In the file Multisheet Workbook, **use the shortcut menu for Sheet1 to rename Sheet1 to** *Australian Division*.	a. **Open the file, Multisheet Workbook.**
	b. **Right-click on Sheet1 and choose Rename.**
🔖 You can also double-click on a sheet tab to rename the sheet tab.	c. **Type** *Australian Division*.
	d. **Press [Enter].**
2. **Rename Sheets 2, 3, 4, and 5** based on the title on each sheet.	a. **Rename Sheet2 as** *European Division*.
	b. **Rename Sheet3 as** *N American Division*.
	c. **Rename Sheet4 as** *S American Division*.
	d. **Rename Sheet5 as** *Summary*.

LESSON 5

3. Use the shortcut menu for the Australian Division sheet tab to change the color of the Australian Division sheet tab to a blue color of your choice.

a. Right-click on the Australian Division sheet tab and choose Tab Color.

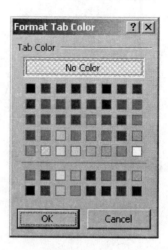

b. In the Format Tab Color dialog box, **select any shade of blue and click OK.**

4. **Change the color of the European Division sheet tab to a shade of green.**

a. **Right-click on the European Division sheet tab and choose Tab Color.**

b. In the Format Tab Color dialog box, **select a shade of green and click OK.**

5. **Change the N American Division sheet tab to a shade of purple, the S American Division sheet tab to a shade of yellow, and the Summary sheet tab to a shade of red.**

a. **Display the shortcut menu for the N American Division sheet tab and choose Tab Color. Select a shade of purple and click OK.**

b. **Display the shortcut menu for the S American Division sheet tab and choose Tab Color. Select a shade of yellow and click OK.**

c. **Display the shortcut menu for the Summary sheet tab and choose Tab Color. Select a shade of red and click OK.**

TOPIC B

Reposition Worksheets in a Workbook

In addition to changing tab colors, another way to organize your worksheet to make it more user-friendly is to reposition your sheet tabs. You will reposition the worksheets by moving the worksheet tabs.

Many Excel workbooks that you create will have multiple worksheets within them. There will most likely be some of those worksheets that you use and refer to more often than others. Wouldn't it be nice if you could make those frequently used worksheets more easily accessible by moving their worksheet tabs to the beginning of the worksheet tabs, rather than having them scattered throughout your workbook? Well, Excel allows you to move worksheets within a workbook, making the frequently used worksheets more easily accessible.

Reposition Worksheets in a Workbook

There are four different ways to reposition worksheets within a workbook. Which way you choose depends on how many worksheets you want to reposition and if they are consecutive or not.

Procedure Reference: Reposition a Single Worksheet

To reposition a single worksheet:

1. Select the worksheet tab.
2. Press and hold the mouse button.
3. Drag the sheet tab until the position indicator is in the desired location.
4. Release the mouse button.

Procedure Reference: Reposition Consecutive Worksheets

To reposition more than one consecutive worksheet:

1. Select the first worksheet.
2. Press and hold down the [Shift] key.
3. Select the last worksheet.
4. Without releasing the mouse button, release [Shift] and drag until the position indicator is in the desired location.
5. Release the mouse button.

Procedure Reference: Reposition Non-consecutive Multiple Worksheets

To reposition multiple worksheets that are not consecutive:

1. Select the first worksheet.
2. Press and hold down the [Ctrl] key.
3. While pressing [Ctrl], select the other worksheets to reposition.
4. Release [Ctrl].

5. Drag the worksheets to the desired location.

6. Release the mouse button.

Procedure Reference: Move a Worksheet from One Workbook to Another

To move a worksheet from one workbook to another:

1. Select the sheet or sheets to be moved.

2. Right-click to display the shortcut menu.

3. Choose Move or Copy.

4. Complete the dialog box information.

5. Click OK.

> When you are moving a worksheet to a new workbook, keep in mind that the worksheet is moved by default. If you wanted to copy, you must specify to copy, rather than move.

ACTIVITY 5-2

Reposition Your Worksheets

Data Files:

- Multisheet Workbook

Setup:

Multisheet Workbook is open.

Scenario:

Now that you have named and added a color to your sheet tabs to organize them, you want to further organize them by re-arranging them. Because you use the N American Division and the European Division sheet tabs the most, you want to place them first in the sheet tabs. You have also been asked by your manager to start a Summary workbook, that will contain the summary information from each department's worksheet. To do this–you will move your Summary worksheet into a new workbook and then the other departments can add their own summary information. When you are finished, your workbook should look like the example shown in Figure 5-2.

| European Division | N American Division | S American Division | **Australian Division** |

Figure 5-2: *Multisheet Workbook after the activity has been completed.*

What You Do	How You Do It
1. Move the Australian Division sheet tab to the right of the European Division sheet tab by dragging.	a. Click on the Australian Division sheet tab and hold down on the mouse button until the mouse pointer changes to an arrow with a piece of paper attached.
	b. Notice to the left of the A in Australian, there is a small down turned arrow. This is the position indicator. Drag the mouse to the right until the position indicator is between the European Division and the N American Division sheet tabs.
	c. Release the mouse button.
2. Select the European Division, Australian Division, and the N American Division sheet tabs and move them to the right of the S American Division sheet tab.	a. Click on the European Division sheet tab. Press the [Shift] key and select the N American Division sheet tab to select multiple sheet tabs.
	b. Drag the three sheet tabs to the right until the position indicator is between the S American sheet tab and the Summary sheet tab.
3. Select the S American Division and the Australian Division and move them to the left of the Summary sheet tab.	a. Click on the S American Division sheet tab.
	b. While pressing the [Ctrl] key, click on the Australian Division sheet tab to select the two non-adjacent sheet tabs.
	c. Click on the Australian Division sheet tab and drag both sheet tabs to the right until the position indicator is between the N American sheet tab and the Summary sheet tab.

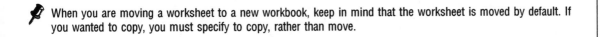

When you are moving a worksheet to a new workbook, keep in mind that the worksheet is moved by default. If you wanted to copy, you must specify to copy, rather than move.

4. Using the shortcut menu, **move the Summary sheet to a new workbook.** Save the new workbook as My Moved Worksheet and close the file.

a. **Right-click on the Summary sheet tab** to display the shortcut menu.

b. **Select Move Or Copy.** The Move Or Copy dialog box is displayed.

c. From the To Book drop-down list, **select (New Book).**

d. **Click OK.** The Summary sheet is moved to a new workbook which is open.

e. **Save the file as** *My Moved Worksheet* and close the file.

TOPIC C

Copy Worksheets

So far, you have changed the color of a worksheet tab and changed the position of a worksheet within a workbook to help organize your workbook. Now you will copy a worksheet to utilize the existing worksheet and start a new department sheet tab.

Have you ever wanted to create a new worksheet and use much of the same data, formatting, and layout of an existing worksheet? Well, when you copy a worksheet, you can use the copied worksheet as a base. You can then make changes to the new worksheet like any other worksheet. This allows you to copy the information from one worksheet and use it in another.

Copy Worksheets

There are two techniques you can use to copy a worksheet. The first can only be used when copying a worksheet within the same workbook. The second technique can be used to copy a worksheet either within the same workbook or to another workbook.

Procedure Reference: Copy a Worksheet within the Same Workbook

To copy a worksheet within the same workbook:

1. Select the worksheet to be copied.

2. Press and hold the [Ctrl] key and drag the sheet tab along the row of tab until the position indicator is pointing to the left of the sheet tab where you want to insert the new sheet.

Procedure Reference: Copy a Worksheet within the Same Workbook or to Another Workbook

To copy a worksheet within the same workbook or to another workbook:

1. Right-click on the sheet you want to copy.

2. Choose Move Or Copy.

3. Complete the dialog box and check Create A Copy.

4. Click OK.

ACTIVITY 5-3

Copy an Existing Worksheet

Setup:

Multisheet Workbook is open.

Scenario:

A new division has been added to your department. There is now a division called the Central American division. Much of the information to be included in the worksheet for this division is the same as the Australian Division worksheet. So, you want to copy the Australian Division worksheet, rename the tab to C American Division, edit the worksheet title to Central American Division, and then delete the data copied from the Australian Division, so you have room to enter the data for the new Central American Division.

	A	B	C	D	E	F	G	H	I
1	**Central American Division**								
2									
3	Item	QTR 1	QTR 2	QTR 3	QTR 4				
4	Hardware	250	300	400	430				
5	Software	560	200	320	200				
6	Furniture	430	290	300	200				
7	Accessories	200	400	500	200				
8									
9	*Totals:*	$1,440	$1,190	$1,520	$1,030				
10									

Tabs: C American Division / European Division / N American Division / S American Division / Australian

Figure 5-3: *Multisheet Workbook after the activity is complete.*

What You Do	How You Do It
1. Use the shortcut menu for the Australian Division tab to copy the Australian Division tab, and paste it to the left of the European Division tab.	a. Select the Australian Division tab and right-click on the tab.
	b. Choose Move Or Copy.
	c. In the Move Or Copy dialog box, **select the Create A Copy box.**
	d. In the Before Sheet list, **select European Division and click OK.**

2. Rename the new worksheet tab *C American Division*.

    a. Right-click on the Australian Division (2) tab.

    b. Choose Rename.

    c. Type *C American Division* and press [Enter].

3. Rename the title on the worksheet *Central American Division* and replace the contents of the totals using Figure 5-3 as a guide. When you are finished, **save the file as** *My Multisheet Workbook*.

    a. Select cell A1. This is the title of the worksheet.

    b. Type *Central American Division* and press [Enter].

    c. Select the range B4:E7 and press [Delete]. The information in the worksheet has been deleted.

    d. Fill in the deleted range using Figure 5-3 as a guide.

    e. Save the file as *My Multisheet Workbook*.

TOPIC D

Change the Number of Worksheets

You now know how to organize your worksheet by changing the color of a worksheet tab, moving a worksheet, and copying a worksheet. It would be useful now to be able to add and delete worksheets to further organize your workbook and make it more user-friendly. You will do just that. In this topic, you will learn how to change the number of worksheets in your workbook by adding and deleting worksheets.

You will often find that when you are working in an Excel workbook, you will need to either add a worksheet or delete an obsolete one. Adding worksheets is something that you will do often when creating a workbook. Deleting worksheets helps to keep your workbook more organized by removing those unused.

Change the Number of Worksheets

Procedure Reference: Insert a Worksheet

To insert a worksheet:

1. Right-click on an existing worksheet.

2. Choose Insert. The new sheet is inserted before the originally selected sheet and becomes the active sheet.

3. Click OK.

Procedure Reference: Delete a Worksheet

To delete a worksheet:

1. Select the sheet to delete.

2. Right-click on the sheet tab.

3. Choose Delete. You will be warned that the sheet will be deleted permanently.

4. Click Delete.

ACTIVITY 5-4

Add and Delete Worksheets

Scenario:

The S. American Division within your department has recently been moved to a different department. Since you have been given the responsibility of updating the department workbook, you need to delete the worksheet that contains the information about this moved division. Your manager has also asked you to add a couple of blank worksheets to the workbook because he is anticipating some additional divisions being added to your department. When you are finished with the activity, your worksheet tabs will look like Figure 5-4.

| C American Division | European Division | N American Division | Australian Division | Sheet1 | **Sheet2** |

Figure 5-4: *The updated workbook pages after the activity is complete.*

What You Do	How You Do It
1. **Use the sheet tab shortcut menu to delete the S American worksheet.**	a. **Select the S American sheet tab.**
	b. **Right-click on the selected sheet tab.**
	c. **Choose Delete.** A warning message is shown, telling you that you are deleting a worksheet that contains data.
	d. **Click Delete.**

2. Add two blank worksheets to the workbook after the Australian Division tab.

   a. **Right-click on the Australian Division sheet tab and choose Insert.** The Insert dialog box appears and allows you to choose a template worksheet to insert.

   b. If necessary, **select Worksheet and click OK.**

   c. **Click on the newly created worksheet and drag it so that it is positioned after the Australian Division tab.**

   d. **Right-click on the Sheet 1 sheet tab.**

   e. **Choose Insert.**

   f. **Click OK.** Your second sheet tab is now inserted.

---

3. **Save and close all files.**

   a. **Choose File→Save.**

   b. **Click the Close button.**

Lesson 5 Follow-up

In this lesson, you have learned how to work with multiple worksheets. First, you learned how to format the worksheet tabs. Then, you learned how to reposition worksheets tabs, copy worksheet tabs, and move worksheet tabs. Finally, you learned how to add and delete worksheets within your workbook.

1. **What are a few reasons you might find it useful to re-arrange and change the number of worksheets within your workbook?**

2. **How will you use the skills you just learned for working with multiple worksheets when you get back to your office?**

NOTES

LESSON 6
Creating and Modifying Charts

Lesson Objectives:

In this lesson, you will create and modify charts.

You will:

* Create a chart.
* Modify chart items.
* Format the chart.
* Change the chart type.

Introduction

So far, you have learned how to work with numerical data in a worksheet. In this lesson, you will learn about using charts to graphically represent your data, thus enhancing your worksheets. You will create a chart, edit the chart's data, modify the chart items, format the chart, and finally change the chart type.

Charts are a very useful visual aid. Have you ever been in a meeting where someone is doing a presentation and is rattling off a lot of numbers? Have you ever thought, "It would really be nice if I could see how the numbers relate"? Charts do just that. They are a graphical representation of numbers and help to show the correlation and relationship between numbers. Using charts in your Excel spreadsheet can help you and others see your data, rather than just read it.

TOPIC A

Create a Chart

You have worked with data in numeric form. Now you will work with your data in graphic form. The first thing you need to do when working with charts is actually create one. In this topic, you will specify the data that you want to portray graphically and create a chart.

Often times, Excel data can be better understood when it is represented graphically. Look at the following figures. Figure 6-1 shows data being displayed numerically. It does tell you what the values are for each group, but determining how the groups are related is more difficult. When you look at the data on the left, you have to draw a mental picture to understand how each of the yearly totals relate to each other. Now look at Figure 6-2. This is giving the same information as the data, but it is easier to understand because it is displayed graphically. You can see how each group relates to each other and how each fits into the whole.

Name	1st Qtr	2nd Qtr	3rd Qtr	4th Qtr		Yr Total
Long	110	175	140	168	$	593
Olson	200	210	240	288	$	938
Stark	300	180	295	354	$	1,129
Unger	220	195	185	222	$	822

Figure 6-1: *Numeric data shown in a worksheet.*

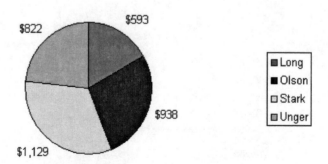

Sales Total for 2000

Figure 6-2: *Graphical representation of numeric data in a worksheet.*

What is a Chart?

One of the tools that Excel offers is the ability to create charts based on existing Excel data.

Definition

A chart in Excel is any graphical representation of data.

Excel Chart Types

There are many different types of charts you can use to represent your data. Table 6-1 describes the different types of charts that you can use to graphically show your data in Excel.

Table 6-1: *The Excel Chart Types and Their Uses*

Chart	Use To
Area	Display the importance of values over time; emphasizes the amount of change, rather than the time or rate of change.
Bar	Display individual values for comparison. Categories are drawn from the vertical axis, and values are drawn from the horizontal axis.
Column	Display individual values for comparison. Categories are drawn from the horizontal axis, and values are drawn from the vertical axis.
Line	Show trends over time; emphasizes time flow and rate of change, rather than the amount of change.
Pie	Display one data series as a whole. Each of its parts represents a percentage of that whole.
Doughnut	Display more than one data series, similar to a pie chart.
Radar	Show changes or frequencies of data relative to a center point and to each other.
XY (Scatter)	Plot coordinate values; shows the relationship between numeric values in several data series.
Bubble	Plot and coordinate values. The size of the data marker indicates the value of a third variable, similar to XY (scatter) charts.
Stock	Display the high, low, and close of stock prices.
3-D Area	Show a three-dimensional view of an area chart.
3-D Bar	Show a three-dimensional view of a bar chart.
3-D Column	Show a three-dimensional view of a column chart.
3-D Line	Show a three-dimensional view of a line chart. Lines appear as bands.
3-D Pie	Show a three-dimensional view of a pie chart.
Surface	Show what appears to be a sheet stretched over the category axis. This chart type is useful for finding the optimum combinations between two sets of data. It's similar to a topographic map; color and pattern indicate areas that are in the same range of values (color doesn't mark the data series).
Cone, Cylinder, and Pyramid	Add a dramatic effect to 3-D column and bar charts.

LESSON 6

Example

Figure 6-3, Figure 6-4, Figure 6-5, and Figure 6-6 show you four different examples of some of the most commonly used charts in Excel.

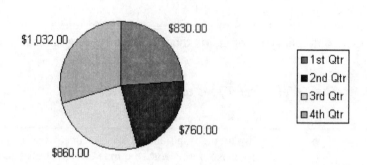

Figure 6-3: *An example of a pie chart.*

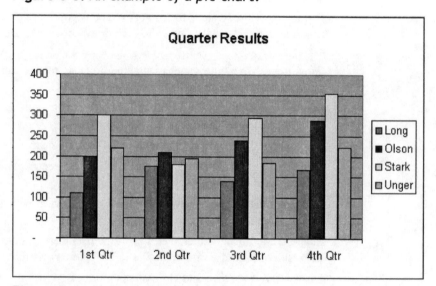

Figure 6-4: *An example of a column chart.*

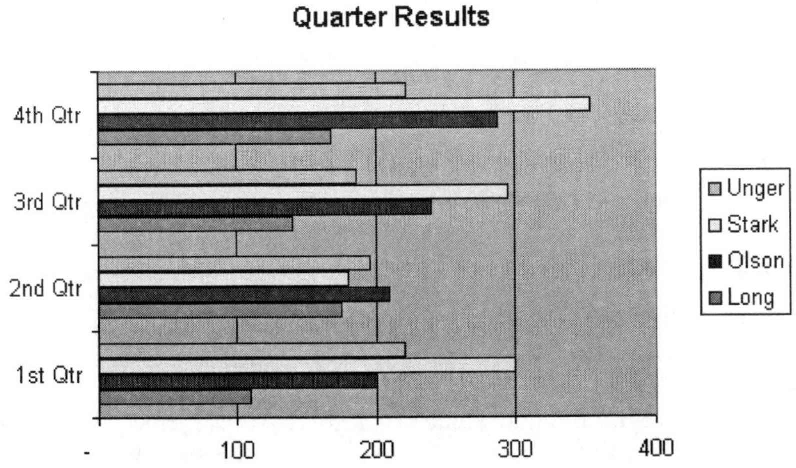

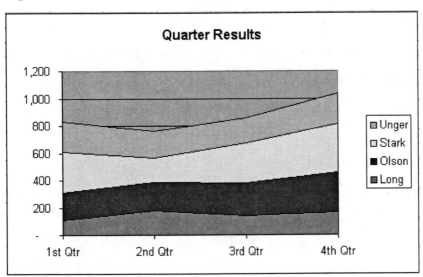

Figure 6-5: *An example of a bar chart.*

Figure 6-6: *An example of an area chart.*

Embedded Charts

When you are creating a chart in Excel, you can also choose to create that chart on an existing worksheet, rather than on a new sheet. This is called an embedded chart.

Chart Sheets

When you create a chart in Excel, you can create your chart on a new sheet within your workbook. This new sheet is called a chart sheet. The only information contained on a chart sheet is the graphic itself.

Create a Chart

Procedure Reference: Create a Chart Using the Chart Wizard

To create a chart based on existing worksheet data using the Chart Wizard:

1. Select the worksheet data to be charted.

✐ The worksheet data you select can include non-adjacent ranges.

2. Click the Chart Wizard button.

3. Use the Chart Wizard to specify the choices for your chart.

✐ The Next button moves you through the Chart Wizard.

Altering Chart Data

Because your charts are based on existing worksheet data, there may come a time when you need to change data values that are linked to a chart. Don't worry. When you edit worksheet data in Excel, if the data value is linked to a chart, the chart is automatically updated with the new value. Therefore, you can edit your chart data in the same way you edit all other Excel data, and you can do this as frequently as you like.

ACTIVITY 6-1

Create a Chart Using Chart Data

Setup:
No files are open.

Scenario:
You are currently working on a worksheet in the file, Chart, located in your My Documents folder. The file contains information about different divisions within your department. You need to pass this workbook along to some other people in your department. Before you do this, you want to create a chart based on the data within your worksheet, so that when others look at it, they can easily interpret the data. You want to create two embedded pie charts—one to show the totals for each quarter and the other to show the totals for each location. You also want to create a column chart on a chart sheet that shows the divisional quarterly sales. When you are done, your pie chart results should match Figure 6-7 and your column charts should match Figure 6-8.

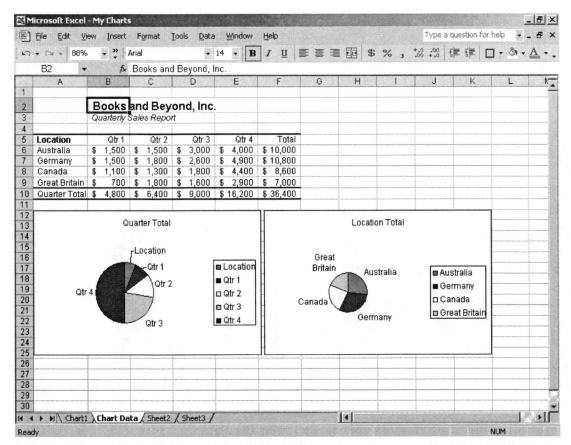

Figure 6-7: *Embedded pie charts showing the totals for each quarter and the totals for each location.*

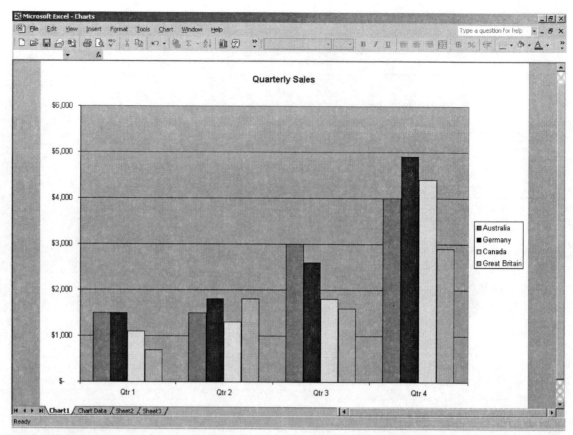

Figure 6-8: *A chart sheet containing a column chart that represents the divisional quarterly sales.*

What You Do   **How You Do It**

 If at any point in the process of creating your charts the Chart toolbar appears, you can close the toolbar by clicking the Close button.

1. In the Charts file, using the Chart Wizard, **create an embedded pie chart that shows the totals for each quarter. Adjust the position of the chart so that it is under the worksheet data.**

a. **Open the file, Charts.**

b. **Select the range A10:E10.**

c. **Click the Chart Wizard** 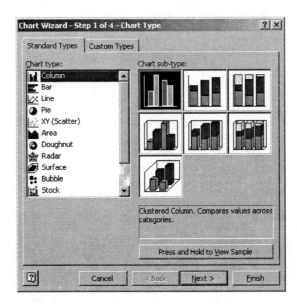 **button.** The first screen of the Chart Wizard appears.

d. In the Chart Type list, **select Pie and click Next.**

e. In the second screen of the Chart Wizard, **select the Series tab.** Next to the Category Labels text box, **click the Select Data Series button** **and select the range B5:E5 and press [Enter]** to designate the column labels as the data labels. **Click Next.**

   As you go through the Chart wizard, watch the preview of the chart to see your updates as you make them.

f. **Click on the Data Labels tab and check the Category Name check box. Click Next.**

g. **Verify that As Object In is selected and click Finish.**

h. **Select the chart and drag the chart below the chart data.**

2. Using the Chart wizard, **create another embedded pie chart that shows the totals for each location.**

a. **Select the range F5:F9.**

b. **Click the Chart Wizard button.** The first screen of the Chart wizard appears.

c. In the Chart Type list, **select Pie and click Next.**

d. **Select the Series tab.**

e. Next to the Category Labels text box, **click the Select Data Series button, select the range A6:A9, and press [Enter]** to designate the row labels as the data labels.

f. **Click Next.**

g. On the Data Labels tab, **check the Category Name check box.**

h. On the Titles tab, in the Chart Title text box, **change the title to *Location Total*.**

i. **Click Next.**

j. **Verify that As Object In is selected and click Finish.**

k. **Select the chart and drag the chart next to the Quarter Total chart.**

3. Create a column chart that shows the data for the divisional quarterly sales on a new sheet. Save the file as *My Charts*.

a. **Select the range A6:E9.**

b. **Click the Chart Wizard button.**

c. In the first screen of the Chart Wizard, **verify that Column is selected as the chart type and click Next.**

d. In the next screen, **select the Series tab.**

e. Next to the Category Labels text box, **click the Fill Data Series button and select the range B5:E5.**

f. **Press [Enter] and click the Next button.**

g. In the third screen of the wizard on the Titles tab, in the Chart Title text box, **type *Quarterly Sales*. Click Next.**

h. To create the chart on a new, blank sheet, **select As New Sheet and click Finish.**

i. **Save the file as *My Charts*.**

TOPIC B

Modify Chart Items

You now know how to create a simple embedded chart and chart sheet to graphically represent your worksheet data. In this topic, you will learn how to modify various chart items to customize your chart and make it as attractive and useful as possible.

Being able to modify chart items is a very useful feature. It allows you to add chart items that you think might be helpful to others, or delete items that you think are distracting and unnecessary. Modifying the chart items is another way to customize your chart so that it serves as the best possible graphical representation of your data. Take a look at the following example. Each chart represents the same data. Notice that the chart in Figure 6-9 is not labeled and it is difficult to know what the chart represents. The chart in Figure 6-10 has a chart title, and a legend, making it easier to understand the data it is supposed to represent.

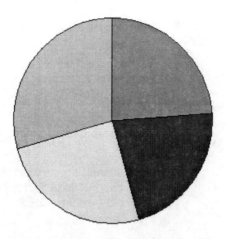

Figure 6-9: *An example of a chart with no chart items.*

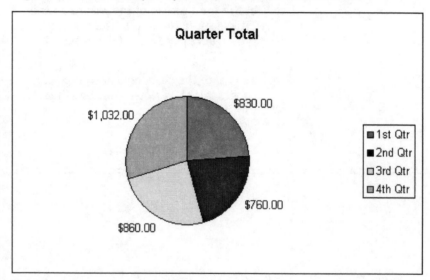

Figure 6-10: *An example of a chart with chart items.*

Chart Terminology

When you create a chart, values from worksheet cells, called *data points* create data markers that can appear as bars, columns, lines, pie slices, or other shapes. A *data marker* is a chart symbol that represents a single data point. All of the data points in a column or row on the worksheet combine on the chart to create a *data series,* which appears on the chart as a group of data markers distinguished by the same color or pattern. For example, all of the entries in the Australia row of the worksheet correspond with the Australia data series of the chart.

A sample of each series' marker color and pattern appears in the legend along with each series' name. The *legend* allows you to identify the series on the chart so that you can easily compare the chart with the worksheet data. The *series name* is simply the title of the row or column in the worksheet where the data was taken.

A typical chart will have two axes, the value axis and the category axis. The *value axis* is typically the vertical axis on the chart. It is also known as the y-axis. Excel plots values for data points against this axis. The *category axis* is typically the horizontal axis on a chart. It is also known as the x-axis. Excel plots category labels along the x-axis, and groups data markers for all series into these categories. If a chart is 3-dimensional, it will also have a z-axis. Gridlines may also be shown on your chart. *Gridlines* are lines that are drawn in the plot area, typically for the value axis, so that data markers can be easily compared with an axis value. Figure 6-11 shows a column chart with callouts pointing to each of these chart components.

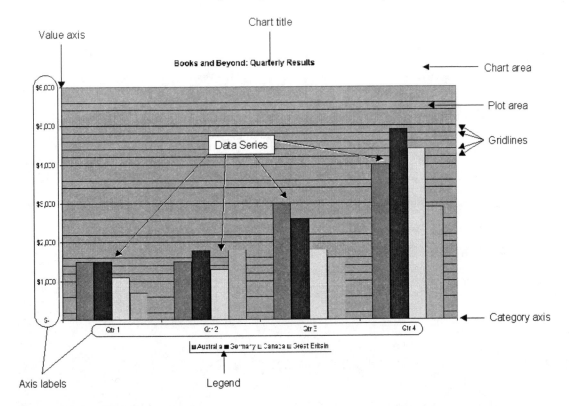

Figure 6-11: *Chart terminology.*

Modify Chart Items

Procedure Reference: Modify Chart Items

To modify chart items:

1. Right-click on the item you want to modify.

2. Choose Format.

> The Format choice will change depending on what item you have selected. For example, if you select the legend, the shortcut menu will be Format Legend. If you right-click on the chart area, the shortcut choice will be Format Chart Area.

ACTIVITY 6-2

Modify Chart Items

Setup:

My Charts is open.

Scenario:

You have decided to make your changes to the column chart that is on the Chart 1 sheet to make it more visually appealing and easier to understand. You want to:

- Change the chart title to Books and Beyond: Quarterly Results.
- Relocate the legend to the bottom of the chart.
- Show both major and minor gridlines.

When you are finished, your chart will look like the example in Figure 6-12.

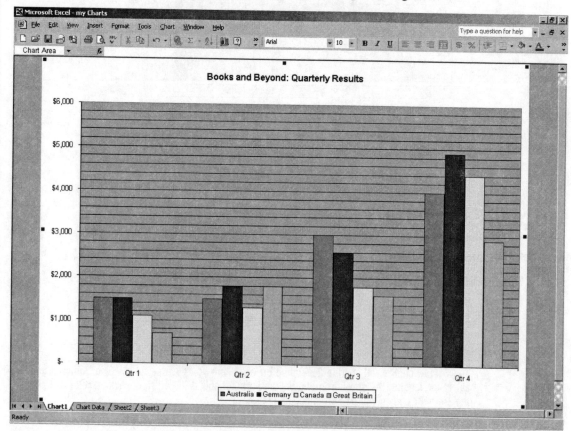

Figure 6-12: *My Charts after the activity has been completed.*

What You Do	How You Do It
1. Change the title of the column chart to *Books and Beyond: Quarterly Results*.	a. Select the Chart 1 sheet.
	b. Choose Chart→Chart Options.
	c. Select the Titles tab.
	d. In the Chart Title text box, **change the title to *Books and Beyond: Quarterly Report*.**
	e. **Click OK.**
2. Change the position of the legend so that it is at the bottom of the chart.	a. **Choose Chart→Chart Options.**
	b. **Select the Legend tab.**
	c. Under Placement, **select Bottom.**

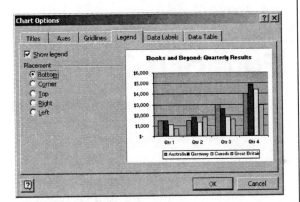

> Notice that you can place the legend in a number of different places in the chart area, and you can also choose to not show the legend.

d. **Click OK.**

3. Show the major and minor gridlines for the value axis. When you are finished, **save the file and compare your chart to the finished sample in the scenario.**

a. **Choose Chart→Chart Options.**

b. **Select the Gridlines tab.**

c. Under Value (Y) Axis, **select Minor Gridlines.** Both Major Gridlines and Minor Gridlines should be selected.

d. **Click OK.**

e. **Click the Save button.**

f. **Compare your finished chart to the sample in** Figure 6-12.

TOPIC C

Format a Chart

After you've finished creating and making modifications to your chart, the next thing you might want to do is to format your chart to make it more visually appealing. In this topic, you will learn how to format a chart.

Formatting charts is another way to modify your chart and make it more professional and attractive. You can add colors and patterns, and modify the font types of your chart. All of this will help you to customize your chart and grab your audience's attention.

Formatting Options

To make your charts more attractive, you can add formatting to chart items. In Excel, you can format all of the chart items. Each chart item has its own set of properties that can be modified. Table 6-2 describes the different formatting options available for charts.

Table 6-2: *Chart Item Formatting Options*

Chart Item	Formatting Options
Chart title	For the chart title, you can change the color, style, size, alignment, and orientation of the text. You can also add a border to the title and change the color, style, weight, shadow effect, and fill effect of the border.
Data labels	For the data labels, you can add a border and change the style, color, weight, shadow effect, and fill effects of that border. You can also adjust the font, font style, font size, font color, background, and effects of the data labels text. You can adjust the number style if the data labels consist of values. Finally, you can adjust the alignment and orientation of the data labels.

Chart Item	Formatting Options
Data series	For the data series, you can add a border and change the style, color, weight, shadow effect, and fill effects of that border. You can also choose to invert the data series if the values are negative. You can plot the series on the primary or secondary axis, adjust the display of the error bars, dictate how your data labels will be shown, and determine the order in which the data series will be displayed on the chart.
Legend	For the legend, you can add a border and change the style, color, weight, shadow effect, and fill effects of that border. You can also adjust the font, font style, font size, font color, background, and effects of the legend text. Also, you can adjust the placement of the legend in the chart area.
Value and category axis	For the value axis, you can adjust the style, color, and weight of the axis lines. You can also determine where the major and minor tick marks will be displayed as well as whether or not to display tick mark labels. You can adjust the scale or range that the axis displays. You can also adjust the font type, style, size, color, and effects of the axis. If the axis is numerical, you can specify the number format and you can also adjust the orientation of the axis.
Gridlines	For the gridlines, you can adjust the line style, color, and weight. You can also adjust the scale and the display units of the gridline.
Chart area	For the chart area, you can add a border and change the line style, color, width of the border, as well as add color fill and change the fill effects of the chart area. Also, you can adjust the font type, style, size, color, and effects of the chart area text. Finally, you can position objects within the chart area.
Plot area	For the plot area, you can add a border and change the line style, color, width of the border, as well as add color fill and change the fill effects of the plot area.

Format a Chart

Procedure Reference: Format a Chart

To format a chart:

1. Choose Chart→Chart Options.

2. Select the tab corresponding to the chart item you want to format.

3. Use the options on the page to make your formatting selections.

4. Click OK.

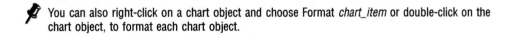 You can also right-click on a chart object and choose Format *chart_item* or double-click on the chart object, to format each chart object.

ACTIVITY 6-3

Format a Chart

Setup:

My Charts is open.

Scenario:

You've created your chart, but looking at it, you decide it's not as visually appealing as it could be. You decide to add formatting to your chart before sending it off to your manager and coworkers. You decide to:

- Add a red, dashed border around the title to draw attention to it.

- Change the font of the axis labels to Times New Roman because you believe it's a more professional looking font.

- Change the fill pattern of the Australian data series to a green pattern.

When you are finished, your worksheet will look like Figure 6-13.

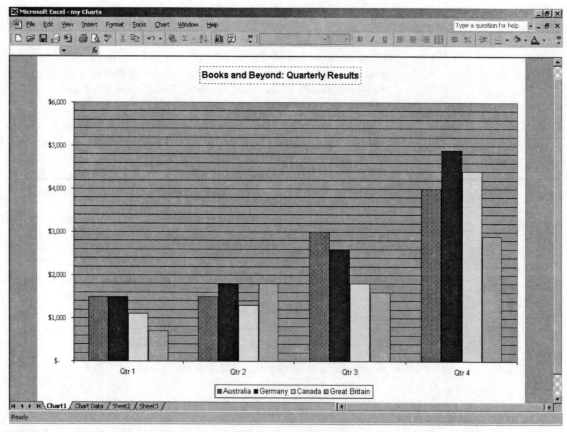

Figure 6-13: *My Charts after the activity is complete.*

What You Do	How You Do It
1. **Add a dashed red line as a border to the chart title.** You can also display the Format dialog box for any chart item by double-clicking on the item.	a. **Right-click on the chart title and choose Format Chart Title.** b. If necessary, **select the Patterns tab.** c. From the Style drop-down list, **select the third selection down from the top.** Notice that you can also change the font and the alignment of the Chart Title in this dialog box. d. **Click on the Color drop-down arrow and select any shade of red.**

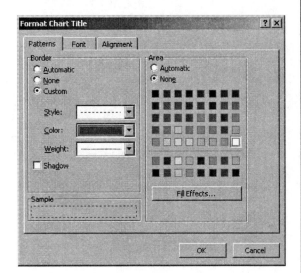

	e. **Click OK.**
2. **Format the value axis labels so they are Times New Roman and blue.**	a. **Double-click on the value axis.** The Format Axis dialog box is displayed. b. **Select the Font tab.**

LESSON 6

c. From the Font list, **scroll down and select Times New Roman.**

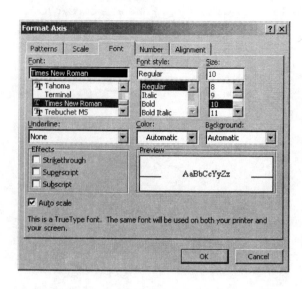

d. From the Color drop-down list, **select any shade of blue.**

e. **Click OK.**

3. **Change the Australia data series fill to green and add a pattern of your choice. Save the file when you are finished and compare your chart to the example shown in Figure 6-13.**

a. **Select the Australia data series** by clicking on the bar graph. **Choose Format→ Selected Data Series.**

b. **Select the Patterns tab.**

c. **Select a shade of green and click Fill Effects.**

d. **Select the Pattern tab, and select a pattern of your choice.**

e. **Click OK twice.**

f. **Save the file and compare it to the example shown in Figure 6-13.**

TOPIC D

Change the Chart Type

In addition to the formatting techniques you've already learned, modifying your chart can include changing its chart type. In this topic, you will change your chart type.

Imagine you have to create a pie chart based on some data in your Excel worksheet. You have some very large data values in your range and some very small data values in the range, making the small data values difficult to read on a pie chart. You need to change the type of chart to one that represents small values along with large values better. You can do this easily in Excel. You can change the type of a chart so that it graphically displays your data in the best way.

Change the Chart Type

Procedure Reference: Change the Type of Your Chart

The chart types available to you when you change a chart type are the same as when you create a chart from scratch. To change the type of your chart:

1. Select the chart.

2. Choose Chart→Chart Type.

3. Select the type of chart you would like.

4. Click OK.

Procedure Reference: Alternate Way to Change the Chart Type

Another way to change the chart type is to:

1. Select the chart and right-click on the chart area.

2. Choose Chart Type and select the type of chart you want to change it to.

3. Click OK.

ACTIVITY 6-4

Changing the Chart Type

Setup:

My Charts is open.

Scenario:

You have created and made changes to your charts. However, you don't think that a column chart is the best way to represent the data in Chart 1. So, you decide to change it to a clustered bar chart. You also want to add a little more flare to the Quarter Total and Location Total pie charts by making them 3-D. Germany had the best location total, so you want to emphasize the Germany pie slice in the Location Total chart by exploding it.

What You Do	How You Do It
1. **Change the column chart on the Chart 1 sheet to a clustered bar chart.**	a. **Select the plot area.** This can be tricky—use the graphic shown as a good way to determine if the Plot Area is selected or not.

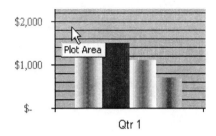

b. **Right-click on the column chart.**

c. **Choose Chart Type.**

d. From the Chart Type list, **select Bar.**

e. In the Chart Sub-type box, **verify that Clustered Bar is selected.**

f. **Click OK.** Your column chart is now a clustered bar chart.

2. Change the Quarter Total pie chart to a 3-D pie chart.

    a. **Select the Chart Data sheet.**

    b. **Right-click on the Quarter Total chart area.**

    c. **Choose Chart Type.**

    d. In the Chart Sub-types section, **select Pie With A 3-D Visual Effect.**

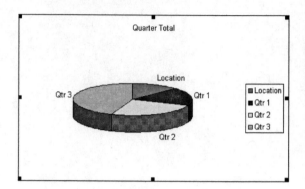

    e. **Click OK.**

3. Change the Location Total pie chart to a 3-D pie chart and make the Germany piece explode from the chart. Save and close the file when you are finished.

a. **Change the Location Total pie chart to a Pie With A 3-D Visual Effect.**

b. **Click on the Germany slice of the pie chart.** The first time you click on it, the whole pie is selected.

c. **Click on the Germany pie slice again** to select just that slice.

d. **Click on the Germany pie slice and drag it away from the pie.** You now have an exploded pie chart.

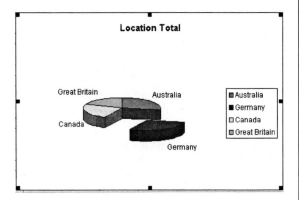

e. **Save the file and then close it.**

Lesson 6 Follow-up

In this lesson, you created a graphical representation of specified data in your worksheet to help show the correlation and relationship between worksheet data by creating both an embedded chart and a chart on a separate chart sheet. You also learned how to make your charts more visually appealing by modifying chart items, formatting the chart and modifying the chart type.

1. **What are some types of data that would benefit from being displayed as a chart?**

2. **What are the three or four types of charts that you think you will use most frequently?**

NOTES

LESSON 7

Setting Page Display and Printing Options

Lesson Objectives:

In this lesson, you will set the page display and printing options.

You will:

*   Freeze rows and columns.

*   Set the print titles.

*   Modify the default page margins.

*   Add a header and footer to your worksheet.

*   Change the page orientation of the worksheets from portrait to landscape.

*   Insert and remove a page break.

*   Specify a print range.

LESSON 7

Introduction

Now that you know how to create and modify your workbook, you need to set the page display and print your worksheet. In this lesson you will freeze and unfreeze rows and columns, set a print title, set the page margins, create a header and footer, change the page orientation, insert and remove a page break, and finally print a range.

You've created a workbook, but unless everyone is going to view your file electronically, you'll want to print it. Before you print your workbook, you need to adjust the printing options. By doing this, you can print parts of all of your worksheets.

TOPIC A

Freeze Rows and Columns

In order to view your workbook easily on screen, you may want to change your page display options. One way to do this is to freeze rows and columns. In this topic, you will learn how to freeze rows and columns to make viewing large amounts of data easier.

Have you ever worked in a worksheet and not been able to see the whole thing on the screen? As you scroll through the data, you are unable to see the column and row information that is at the top of the worksheet. There will come a time when you are working in Excel that you will work with a worksheet that is too large to fit the screen. When the worksheet is too large to fit on the screen it is helpful to freeze rows and columns to keep headings and titles within view as you work with large amounts of data.

Freeze Rows and Columns

Procedure Reference: Freeze Columns or Rows

To freeze columns or rows:

1. Select a cell in the row and/or column that is below or to the right of the rows and/or columns you want to freeze.

2. Choose Window→Freeze Panes.

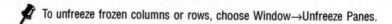 To unfreeze frozen columns or rows, choose Window→Unfreeze Panes.

ACTIVITY 7-1

Freezing and Unfreezing Columns and Rows

Data Files:

• Page Display

Setup:

No files are open.

Scenario:

You need to make some changes to your worksheet, so you will be doing a lot of viewing on screen. Your worksheet contains several screens full of data, so to make viewing easier, you want to be able to view the column headings at all times, even as you scroll down through the worksheet. So, you decide to freeze the column heading row and everything above so that, as you move through your data, your headings are always in view.

What You Do	How You Do It
1. In the file Page Display, **freeze the top four rows in your worksheet.**	a. **Select cell A5.**
	b. **Choose Window→Freeze Panes.**
	Notice the black line that appears, indicating where the panes are frozen.
2. **Experiment navigating through your data.** **What do you notice about your headings?**	
3. **Unfreeze the panes. Save the file as** *My Page Display* **when you are finished.**	a. **Scroll through the data and observe how the panes have been frozen.**
	b. **Choose Window→Unfreeze Panes.**
	c. **Save the file as** *My Page Display.*

TOPIC B

Set Print Title

Freezing columns and rows as a header is a display option only. Once you are ready to print your document, you may want to set some print titles. In this topic, you will set print titles for your columns and rows.

Have you ever had a printed worksheet that is multiple pages? Have you ever had a multi-page worksheet where the header rows are not printed on every page, so you have to keep referring back to the first page to find out what each column and row contains? This can be very annoying if you want to look something up on a printed worksheet quickly. Setting print titles will prevent this from happening. By setting print titles, you can print the column and row header on every page so that they are always there for reference.

What is a Print Title?

A print title is a specified range of cells that print at the top of every page or at the left of every page. Typically, you will use this if your worksheet has multiple pages and you want the column or row heading to appear on every printed page.

Set Print Title

Procedure Reference: Set Print Titles for a Worksheet

To set print titles for your worksheet:

1. Choose File→Page Setup.

2. Select the Sheet tab.

3. Using the selection indicator next to the Rows To Repeat At Top text box, select the rows you want to set as your print title.

    You can also set columns for print titles by using the Columns To Repeat At Left option.

4. Press Enter.

5. Click OK.

ACTIVITY 7-2

Setting Print Titles

Setup:

My Page Display is open.

Scenario:

Your worksheet is multiple pages. You want to print all the pages so that your column headings repeat on every page. You decide to set the first row in your worksheet as the print title.

What You Do	How You Do It
1. If necessary, **set the Print Title to the range A4:E4.**	a. **Choose File→Page Setup.**
	b. **Select the Sheet tab.**
	c. **Click on the selection indicator next to the Rows To Repeat At Top text box.**
	d. **If necessary, click on cell A4. Press [Enter].** The Print Title has been set.

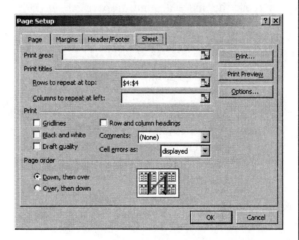

2. Preview the worksheet to verify that your print titles are set. When you are finished, save the file.

   a. Click the Print Preview button.

   b. **Scroll through the spreadsheet.** Row 4 is repeated on every page.

   c. **Click the Close button** to exit from Print Preview.

   d. **Save the file.**

TOPIC C

Set Page Margins

Now that you have print titles set, you might want to alter your worksheet's page margins to increase or decrease the amount of data that prints on each page.

Have you ever printed a worksheet and wanted to see more blank space surrounding the worksheet for taking notes? Adjusting the margins would allow this. You can increase and decrease the space around the worksheet data by adjusting your margins.

What is a Margin?

A margin determines the amount of space between the worksheet data and the edge of the paper. There are six adjustable margins. The right and left margins determine the amount of space at the right and left edge of the paper. The top and bottom margins determine the amount of space at the top and bottom of the page. The last two margins, the header and footer margins, determine the amount of space between the header or footer and the body of the worksheet printout. An example is shown in Figure 7-1.

Sheet1

Books and Beyond - All Divisions
International Sales Meeting

Australian Division

Name	January	February	March	April	May	June	July
Long, Albe	110	175	140	145	140	160	140
Olson, Lawrence	200	210	240	240	240	240	240
Stark, Thomas	300	180	295	260	295	230	295
Unger, Angela	220	195	185	185	185	185	185
TOTAL:	$830	$760	$860	$830	$860	$815	$860
AVERAGE:	$208	$190	$215	$208	$215	$204	$215
HIGH:	$300	$210	$295	$260	$295	$240	$295

European Division

Name	January	February	March	April	May	June	July
Kraft, Christopher	306	195	203	145	140	160	140
Oakes, Phillip	219	147	137	240	240	240	240
Rider, Matthew	104	230	185	260	295	230	295
Sweet, Stephanie	125	100	206	185	170	175	180
Wilson, Bridgette	320	255	235	240	245	250	255
TOTAL:	$754	$672	$731	$830	$845	$805	$855
AVERAGE:	$189	$168	$183	$208	$211	$201	$214
HIGH:	$306	$230	$206	$260	$295	$240	$295

South American Division

Name	January	February	March	April	May	June	July
Marquez, Fernandez	150	185	150	145	140	160	140
Hernandez, Ricardo	220	220	220	240	240	240	240
Flores, Bridgette	275	175	275	260	295	230	295
Diego, Annette	210	185	195	185	170	175	180
TOTAL:	$855	$765	$840	$830	$845	$805	$855

Page 1

Figure 7-1: *An example of a worksheet with 1 1/2 inch top and bottom margins.*

Set Page Margins

Procedure Reference: Change the Page Margins in Print Preview

You can change the page margins from the Print Preview window by:

1. Clicking the Margins button.

🖈 The margins appear as lines on the worksheet preview.

2. Dragging the margin lines to the desired location.

Procedure Reference: Change the Margins Using the Page Setup Dialog Box

You can also change the margins using the Page Setup dialog box by:

1. Choosing File→Page Setup.

2. Selecting the Margins tab.

3. Adjusting each margin number as desired.

ACTIVITY 7-3

Setting Your Page Margins

Setup:
My Page Display is open.

Scenario:
You have created, formatted, and edited the My Page Display workbook, and now you would like to print it. You want to distribute this worksheet during a meeting and you've decided to increase the amount of whitespace on the printed worksheet so that people can make notes right on the page. You decide to provide 1 1/2 inches of margin space at the bottom of the page for notes. You realize that increasing the bottom whitespace takes away from the amount of space available for data to print on each individual page. You decide to decrease the right and left margins to a quarter of an inch to make up for the increased margin at the bottom of the page.

What You Do	How You Do It
1. Use the Page Setup dialog box to adjust the left and right margins to 1/4".	a. **Click the Print Preview button.**
	b. In the Print Preview window, **click the Setup button.**
	c. **Select the Margins tab.**
	d. **Select the number in the Left margin text box and type** *0.25*.
	e. **Press the [Tab] key, and type** *0.25* **to change the right margin.**
	f. **Click OK.** Your left and right margins are now smaller and more of your information fits on one page.

2. Use the Margin Guide indicators to **adjust the bottom margin so that there is about 1 1/2 inches of space at the bottom for taking notes.**

a. In the Print Preview window, **click the Margins button.** The Margin Guide indicators are displayed.

b. **Place your mouse pointer over the line that is second from the bottom. This is** the bottom margin.

c. **Click and hold your mouse button.** Notice that the status bar indicates that you have selected the bottom margin and it also specifies the margin's location. Drag the bottom border up until the indicator displays about 1.5.

Bottom Margin: 1.51

d. **Release the mouse button.**

3. **Close the Print Preview window and save the file.**

a. **Click the Close button** to close the Print Preview window.

b. **Save the file.**

TOPIC D

Create a Header and Footer

In addition to setting print titles for your data that will print on every page, you can also create headers and footers that are displayed in the top and bottom margins.

Have you ever wanted to put the date at the top of your worksheet? How about adding page numbers to a multi-page worksheet? These are both examples of headers and footers.

Headers and Footers

A header and footer consist of text that prints at the top and bottom of each page of your workbook. The header prints at the top, while the footer prints at the bottom. Headers and footers contain three sections. The first section aligns its contents with the left edge of the page; the second section centers its contents on the page; and the third section aligns its contents with the right edge of the page. Figure 7-2 shows an example of what a header and footer look like in Print Preview.

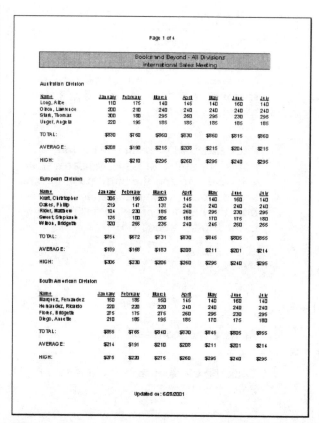

Figure 7-2: *An example of a worksheet with a header and footer.*

Create a Header and Footer

Procedure Reference: Insert a Header or Footer into a Worksheet

To insert a header or footer into an Excel worksheet:

1. Display the Page Setup dialog box. (Choose File→Page Setup.)

2. Select the Header/Footer tab.

3. To create a custom header or footer:

    A. Click the Custom Header or Custom Footer button.

    B. Place your insertion point in the section you want the header or footer text to appear.

    C. Type text and click OK twice.

4. To insert an existing header or footer:

    A. Display the Header or Footer drop-down list.

    B. Select the header or footer text you want.

    C. Click OK.

ACTIVITY 7-4

Creating a Header and Footer

Setup:

My Page Display is open.

Scenario:

Your data is time-sensitive and you want to print the date on the top of your printed pages so that everyone knows the date the printout was generated. You think it would be useful to also add your name since you will be handing this worksheet out to co-workers at a meeting. Then they will know who created it. You decide to add a header with a centered date and a footer with your name left-aligned and the page number right-aligned.

What You Do	How You Do It
1. **Add a custom header that contains the date information in the center of the header.**	a. **Click the Print Preview button.**
	b. In the Print Preview window, **click the Setup button.**
	c. **Select the Header/Footer tab.**
	d. **Click Custom Header.**
	e. **Place the insertion point in the Center Section text box.**
	f. **Click the Date button** 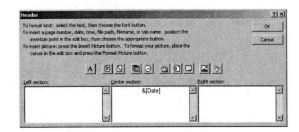 .
	g. **Click OK.** Notice that the date appears in the Header preview section.
2. **Add a custom footer that contains your name left-aligned and the page number right-aligned. When you are finished, save the file.**	a. **Click Custom Footer.**
	b. With the insertion point in the Left Section text box, **type your name.**

c. **Place the insertion point in the Right Section text box and click the Page Number button** 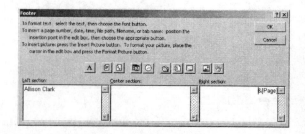 .

d. **Click OK.** Notice the footer preview section.

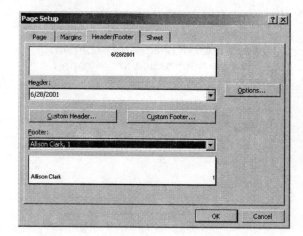

e. **Click OK** to close the Page Setup dialog box and apply the header and footer. Notice that they now appear in the preview window.

f. **Close Print Preview and save the file.**

TOPIC E

Change Page Orientation

You are getting ready to print your worksheet. One more thing you need to do is to check that page orientation is appropriate to display your data. In this topic, you will change the page orientation of your worksheet.

Have you ever had a worksheet that was wider than it was long? Or, has your worksheet been longer than it is wide? Both of these situations can lead to an ugly printout, unless you adjust the page orientation.

Available Orientations

There are two types of page orientation you can choose from in Excel. The first is Portrait. This will display the data with the paper positioned vertically. The other is Landscape, where the paper is positioned horizontally. Figure 7-3 shows the options in the Page Setup dialog box.

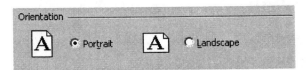

Figure 7-3: *Page orientation options.*

Change Page Orientation

Procedure Reference: Change the Page Orientation of a Worksheet

To change the page orientation of your worksheet:

1. Display the Page Setup dialog box.

2. On the Page tab, under Orientation, select the desired page orientation.

Page Setup Options

In addition to being able to change the page orientation of a worksheet, there are other options you may want to use when printing a worksheet. Table 7-1 displays some of the common options you can use when setting up a worksheet to print.

Table 7-1: *Common Page Setup Options*

Option	Tab	What It Does	To Use
Scaling	Page	Scales a worksheet to a specified dimension or percentage for printing.	Select the radio button corresponding to the scaling option you want to use and select the dimension or percentage of scaling you want to apply.
Print Area	Sheet	Prints only a specified area of a worksheet.	In the Print area section of the Sheet tab of the Page Setup dialog box, select only the range of cells that you want to print.

Option	Tab	What It Does	To Use
Repeat Rows or Columns	Sheet	Prints a specified row or column on every page of a worksheet's print out.	In the Print titles section of the Sheet tab of the Page Setup dialog box, select the column and/or row that you want to print on every worksheet.
Setting Gridlines to Print	Sheet	Prints the gridlines of a worksheet.	Check the Gridlines check box.

> You can also set the Print Area of a worksheet by choosing File→Print Area and setting the area.

ACTIVITY 7-5

Changing the Page Orientation

Setup:

My Page Display is open and all previous activities have been completed.

Scenario:

You are ready to print your document, but when you preview it, you notice that the worksheet data is too wide to fit on the page. You want to change the orientation of your page from Portrait to Landscape to solve this problem.

What You Do	How You Do It
1. Change the page orientation to Landscape.	a. Choose File→Page Setup.
	b. Select the Page tab.
	c. Under Orientation, select Landscape.
	d. Click OK.
2. Preview the document and then save the file.	a. Click the Print Preview button.
	b. Scroll through the worksheet. Notice the changes that have been made.
	c. Click the Close button.
	d. Save the file.

TOPIC F

Insert and Remove Page Breaks

You've learned how to control printing from the stand point of adding additional components to your printout. In this topic, you are going to insert some page breaks into your worksheet to control how much data prints on each page.

You have a worksheet that has multiple pages. The only problem is that the pages are breaking in places that you don't want them to, separating data that really needs to stay together. By inserting your own page breaks, you can control where the pages are broken.

What is a Page Break?

When a worksheet printout is too large to fit on one piece of paper, Excel inserts automatic page breaks based on paper size, margin settings, and scaling options in the Page Setup dialog box. If you don't like where the automatic page breaks separate your data, you can insert your own page breaks, which are called manual page breaks.

Insert and Remove a Page Break

Procedure Reference: Adjust a Page Break while in Print Preview

To adjust a page break while in Print Preview:

1. Click the Page Break Preview button.

2. Drag the page break to the correct row.

Procedure Reference: Insert Page Breaks Directly into a Worksheet

To insert page breaks directly into the worksheet:

1. Select the cell in column A, or an entire row, that you want to print on the new page.

2. Choose Insert→Page Break. A dashed line appears above the row of the selected cell.

Procedure Reference: Remove a Page Break

To remove a page break:

1. Select the cell or row that was selected to create the page break.

2. Choose Insert→Remove Page Break.

ACTIVITY 7-6

Adding and Deleting Page Breaks

Setup:
My Page Display is open and all previous activities have been completed.

Scenario:
You have a worksheet that has multiple pages. The automatic page breaks Excel uses areseparating data that needs to be printed together. You decide that the page needs to be broken before row 31 or perhaps row 28. You aren't quite sure which would look best when it prints. You decide to try both and see which one you like best.

What You Do	How You Do It
1. **Insert a page break before row 31** using the Insert menu.	a. **Select cell A31.**
	b. **Choose Insert→Page Break.** Notice the dotted line that indicates a page break.
2. **Delete the page break you inserted.**	a. **Choose Insert→Remove Page Break.**
3. Using the Print Preview window, **preview the page breaks and adjust them so that there is a page break after row 28.**	a. **Display the Print Preview window.**
	b. **Click the Page Break Preview button.**
	c. If necessary, in the Welcome To Page Break Preview window, **check the Do Not Show This Dialog Box Again check box and click OK.**
	d. **Click on the blue horizontal line and drag it up until it is below row 28.**
	e. **Choose View→Normal.**
4. **Preview the file** and see the effect your new page break has. **Save the file** when you are finished.	a. **Click the Print Preview button.**
	b. **Scroll through the spreadsheet.**
	c. **Close Print Preview.**
	d. **Save the file.**

TOPIC G

Print a Range

You've learned how to prepare for and print an entire worksheet in Excel. Now you're ready to learn how to print just a portion of a worksheet.

Have you ever wanted to print part of a worksheet, but not the whole thing? Because worksheets can sometimes be very long and full of data, at some point you may want to print only a section of a worksheet. Specifying a print range allows you to print only a specific area of your worksheet.

Print a Range

Procedure Reference: Specify a Print Area Using the Print Dialog Box

There are two ways you can specify an area to print. The first way to specify a print area is to:

1. Select the area you want to print on your worksheet.

2. Choose File→Print.

3. In the Print What box, select Selection.

Procedure Reference: Specify a Print Area Using the Page Setup Dialog Box

The second way to specify a print area is to:

1. Choose File→Page Setup.

2. Select the Sheet tab.

3. Next to the Print Area text box, click on the selection indicator.

4. Select the area you want to print and press [Enter]. This will remain the print area until you change it or delete it.

ACTIVITY 7-7

Setting and Printing a Print Range

Setup:

My Page Display is open and all previous activities have been completed.

Scenario:

Now you are ready to print your worksheet for that important meeting. However, you don't want to print the whole worksheet and overwhelm your audience with data they don't care about. You decide just to print the range containing the critical data for the meeting—A1:H31.

What You Do	How You Do It
1. Using the Page Setup dialog box, **set the print area to the range A1:H31.**	a. **Choose File→Page Setup.**
You can also set a print area by selecting the area you want to print in the worksheet and choosing File→Print. Then, under Print What, select Selection and click OK.	b. **Select the Sheet tab.**
	c. Next to the Print Area text box, **click on the selection indicator.**
	d. **Select the range A1:H31 and press [Enter].**

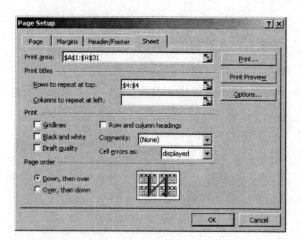

2. **Begin the process of printing the worksheet, but cancel the action before you print. Save and close the file.**	a. **Click the Print button.**

b. **Notice the options in the Print dialog box.** You can specify how many copies you want to print, which range to print, and then you can preview your worksheet from the Print dialog box.

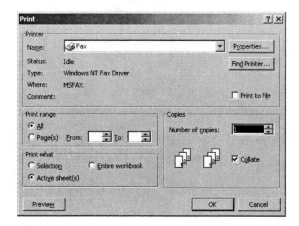

c. **Click OK.**

d. **Save and close the file.**

Lesson 7 Follow-up

In this lesson, you learned how to set the page display and printing options so that you can print your Excel workbooks. You learned how to freeze and unfreeze rows and columns for display purposes to help you navigate within data that covers more than one screen. To set up for printing, you set the print title, changed the margins, and set the header and footer. You made final modifications for printing by changing the page orientation, and inserting and removing page breaks. You then learned how to print just a small portion of your data instead of the entire workbook.

1. **What are some of the page display options that you will find most useful back at your office and why?**

2. **What techniques for preparing a worksheet for printing have you learned that you think will be most useful to you?**

Follow-up

In this course, you learned how to create basic worksheets and charts. You now have the skills you need to enter, edit, format, and perform calculations on data. You can work with multiple worksheets and set page display and printing options. In addition, you can create, edit, and format charts. Now, when you create your worksheets, it should be quick and easy.

What's Next?

Now that you've mastered the basics of Excel 2002, you may want to consider delving further into this software's capabilities, features, and uses. You'll find all of that and more in *Excel 2002: Level 2*.

APPENDIX A

Common Problems Associated with Printing

As with any program, what you get from the printer may not be what you expected to get. Table A-2 displays some common problems you may encounter when printing Excel worksheets and how to fix them.

 You can get a complete list of printing problems and their fixes by choosing Help→Microsoft Excel Help and searching on the keyword Troubleshoot Printing.

Table A-2: *Common Problems Associated with Printing Excel Worksheets*

Problem	How to Fix

Nothing happens when you print the document	• Ensure that there is a printer setup in Windows.
	• Check to make sure you have a printer selected in Excel.
	   • Choose File→Print.
	   • Select the printer you want to use.

Only a portion of a worksheet prints	Check to see if a print area is defined. If it is, clear the print area by choosing File→Print Area→Clear Print Area.
Excel prints too may rows or columns	To control how many rows or columns Excel prints, make sure a print area is defined in the Page Setup dialog box.
The worksheet header or footer prints incorrectly	• Use black and white text only. • In the Page Setup dialog box, verify that the header or footer is defined as you desire.
Repeating rows and columns do not print on some pages	Make sure you have selected a range of cells to repeat in the Page Setup dialog box and that you are printing cells other than those used as the labels.

APPENDIX A

Problem	How to Fix
Excel ignores page breaks	• Make sure you have not chosen to scale your worksheet based on a specified number of pages. • Use Adjust To scaling instead of Fit To scaling to maintain page breaks. • Set each page as a separate print area.
Some columns or rows print on the wrong page	• In the Page Setup dialog box, decrease the page margins. • In the Page Setup dialog box, select the Fit To scaling option to make the extra columns or rows fit on the desired page. • In the Page Setup dialog box, change the paper orientation to fit mor rows or columns. • In the worksheet, adjust page breaks.

APPENDIX B

Microsoft Office Specialist Program

Selected Element K courseware addresses Microsoft Office Specialist skills. The following tables indicate where Excel 2002 skills are covered. For example, 1-3 indicates the lesson and activity number applicable to that skill.

Core Skill Sets and Skills Being Measured	Excel 2002: Level 1	Excel 2002: Level 2	Excel 2002: Level 3
Working with Cells and Cell Data			
Insert, delete, and move cells	2-1, 2-6, 4-10		
Enter and edit cell data including text, numbers, and formulas	1-2, 1-4, 2-6, 3-1, 3-3, 3-5, 3-6, 4-1, 4-2, 4-3, 4-4, 4-5, 4-6, 4-7, 4-8, 4-9, 4-10, 4-11		
Check spelling		1-4	
Find and replace cell data and formats	2-7, 4-7, 4-10		
Work with a subset of data by filtering lists		2-4	
Managing Workbooks			
Manage workbook files and folders	1-6, 2-1		
Create workbooks using templates		1-1	
Save workbooks using different names and file formats	1-2, 1-6, 3-1		
Formatting and Printing Worksheets			
Apply and modify cell formats	1-5, 4-1, 4-2, 4-3, 4-4, 4-5, 4-6, 4-7, 4-8, 4-9, 4-10, 4-11		
Modify row and column settings	2-4, 7-1	3-3	

Appendix B

Core Skill Sets and Skills Being Measured	Excel 2002: Level 1	Excel 2002: Level 2	Excel 2002: Level 3
Modify row and column formats	4-8, 4-9		
Apply styles	4-4		
Use automated tools to format worksheets	4-11		
Modify Page Setup options for worksheets	7-2, 7-3, 7-4, 7-5, 7-7		
Preview and print worksheets and workbooks	7-7	3-1	
Modifying Workbooks			
Insert and delete worksheets	5-4		
Modify worksheet names and positions	5-1, 5-2		
Use 3-D references		4-1	
Creating and Revising Formulas			
Create and revise formulas	3-1, 3-2, 3-3, 3-5, 3-6		
Use statistical, data and time, financial, and logical functions in formulas	3-1, 3-3	4-3, 4-5	
Creating and Modifying Graphics			
Create, modify, position and print charts	6-1, 6-3		
Create, modify and position graphics		1-3	
Workgroup Collaboration			
Convert worksheets into web pages		3-4	
Create hyperlinks		6-1	
View and edit comments		6-2, 6-3, 6-4	

Expert Skill Sets And Skills Being Measured	Excel 2002: Level 1	Excel 2002: Level 2	Excel 2002: Level 3
Importing and Exporting Data			
Import data to Excel		3-1, 3-2	
Export data from Excel		3-3	
Publish worksheets and workbooks to the Web		3-5	
Managing Workbooks			
Create, edit, and apply templates		1-2, 1-3, 1-4	
Create workspaces			2-1
Use Data Consolidation			2-2, 2-4
Formatting Numbers			

Expert Skill Sets And Skills Being Measured	Excel 2002: Level 1	Excel 2002: Level 2	Excel 2002: Level 3
Create and apply custom number formats	4-2		
Use conditional formats			1-1
Working with Ranges			
Use named ranges in formulas		4-2	
Use Lookup and Reference functions		4-4	
Customizing Excel			
Customize toolbars and menus			1-3, 1-4
Create, edit, and run macros			1-5, 1-7
Auditing Worksheets			
Audit formulas		4-6, 4-7	
Locate and resolve errors		4-8	
Identify dependencies in formulas		4-6, 4-7, 4-8	
Summarizing Data			
Use subtotals with lists and ranges		2-3	
Define and apply filters		2-5	
Add group and outline criteria to ranges			1-7
Use data validation			1-2
Retrieve external data and create queries			2-7
Create Extensible Markup Language (XML) Web queries			2-9
Analyzing Data			
Create PivotTables, PivotCharts, and PivotTable/PivotChart Reports		5-1, 5-2	
Forecast values with *what-if* analysis		4-4	
Create and display scenarios		5-3	
Workgroup Collaboration			
Modify passwords, protections, and properties			3-1, 3-2
Create a shared workbook			3-3
Track, accept, and reject changes to workbooks			3-4, 3-7
Merge workbooks			3-6

NOTES

APPENDIX C

Internet and Computing Core Certification (IC³) Program

Module 2 (Key Applications) Objectives

The Internet and Computing Core Certification (IC³) program consists of three modules—Computing Fundamentals, Key Applications, and Living Online—and is intended for candidates who seek certification in the areas of computer hardware, software, networks and the Internet. Individuals must pass three exams, one associated with each module, in order to earn IC³ certification.

Selected Element K courseware addresses module-specific objectives. The following table indicates where Module 2 (Key Applications) objectives are covered in Element K courseware. For example, 1A indicates that the applicable objective is addressed in Lesson 1, Topic A.

IC³ Module 2 (Key Applications) Objectives	Excel 2002: Level 1 (084200)	Excel 2002: Level 2 (084201)	Word 2002: Level 1 (084300)	Word 2002: Level 2 (084301)
1.1 Be able to start and exit a Windows application and utilize sources of online help				
1.1.1 Start a Windows application	1B			
1.1.2 Exit a Windows application	1E			
1.1.3 Identify and prioritize help resources (online, documentation, help desk, etc.)	1F		1D	
1.1.4 Access online help	1F		1D	
1.1.5 Use help search functionality	1F		1D	
1.1.6 Access Internet-based help functionality			1D	
1.2 Identify common on-screen elements of Windows applications, change application settings and manage files within an application				

Appendix C

IC³ Module 2 (Key Applications) Objectives		Excel 2002: Level 1 (084200)	Excel 2002: Level 2 (084201)	Word 2002: Level 1 (084300)	Word 2002: Level 2 (084301)
1.2.1	Identify on-screen elements common to Windows applications (pull-down menus, toolbars, scroll bars, title bar, status bar, application window, document windows, mouse pointer, etc.)	1B		1A	
1.2.2	Display or hide toolbars			5C	
1.2.3	Switch between open documents			2C	
1.2.4	Change views			1A	
1.2.5	Change magnification level			7D	
1.2.6	Create new files			1A	
1.2.7	Create new files based on pre-existing templates			6A	
1.2.8	Open files			2A	
1.2.9	Save files			1B	
1.2.10	Save files in different locations, names, file formats			1B	
1.2.11	Identify and solve common problems relating to working with files (identify why files cannot be opened, resolve file incompatibility issues, etc.)			1B	
1.3	Perform common editing and formatting functions				
1.3.1	Navigate around open files with scroll bars, keyboard shortcuts, or the Go command			2B	
1.3.2	Select information			2B	
1.3.3	Clear selected information	2D			
1.3.4	Cut selected information			2C	
1.3.5	Copy selected information			2C	
1.3.6	Paste cut or copied information			2C	
1.3.7	Use the Undo, Redo and Repeat commands			2C	
1.3.8	Find information			6E	
1.3.9	Replace information			6E	
1.3.10	Check spelling			6F	
1.3.11	Change fonts			3B	
1.3.12	Bold, underline, italicize text			3A	
1.3.13	Change text color			3C	

IC³ Module 2 (Key Applications) Objectives		Excel 2002: Level 1 (084200)	Excel 2002: Level 2 (084201)	Word 2002: Level 1 (084300)	Word 2002: Level 2 (084301)
1.3.14	Apply text effects (super-script, subscript, etc.)			3A	
1.3.15	Change text orientation (left, right, center, justify)			4A	
1.4	Perform common printing functions				
1.4.1	Set margins			7D	
1.4.2	Change paper size and orien-tation			7B	
1.4.3	Preview a file before printing			7A	
1.4.4	Print files			7G	
1.4.5	Use common printing options (number of pages, number of copies, printer, etc.)			7G	
1.4.6	Identify and solve problems associated with printing	Appendix A		Appendix A	
2.1	Be able to format text and documents including the ability to use automatic formatting tools				
2.1.1	Change line spacing and paragraph spacing			4B	
2.1.2	Indent text			4E	
2.1.3	Create bulleted and num-bered lists			4F	
2.1.4	Insert symbols			6C	
2.1.5	Use, modify and delete tabs			4D	
2.1.6	Insert a page break or section break			7E	
2.1.7	Insert, modify and format page numbers			7C	
2.1.8	Create, modify and format headers and footers			7E	
2.1.9	Apply borders and shading to text paragraphs			4C	
2.1.10	Create and apply styles				1A
2.1.11	Apply AutoFormats (themes)				6E
2.1.12	Use the Format Painter				
2.1.13	Use AutoText			1C	
2.2	Be able to add tables and graphics to documents				
2.2.1	Create a table			5A	
2.2.2	Select rows and columns			5B	
2.2.3	Insert rows and columns			5B	
2.2.4	Delete rows and columns			5B	
2.2.5	Split cells			5B	
2.2.6	Merge cells				2B

IC³ Module 2 (Key Applications) Objectives		Excel 2002: Level 1 (084200)	Excel 2002: Level 2 (084201)	Word 2002: Level 1 (084300)	Word 2002: Level 2 (084301)
2.2.7	Change column width and row height			5B	
2.2.8	Split tables			5A	
2.2.9	Format tables with borders and shading			5C	
2.2.10	Automatically format tables with AutoFormat			5D	
2.2.11	Insert pictures into a document				3A
2.2.12	Modify pictures in a document				3A
2.2.13	Add drawn objects into a document				3B
2.2.14	Manipulate drawn objects in a document				3B
3.1	Be able to modify worksheet data and structure				
3.1.1	Insert data into cells	1B			
3.1.2	Modify data in cells	1C			
3.1.3	Fill cells	2C			
3.1.4	Insert and delete cells	2D			
3.1.5	Insert and delete rows and columns	2D			
3.1.6	Insert and delete worksheets	5D			
3.1.7	Adjust column width and row height	4G			
3.1.8	Adjust column width using AutoFit	4G			
3.1.9	Hide and unhide rows and columns		3C		
3.2	Be able to sort data and manipulate data using formulas and functions				
3.2.1	Sort worksheet data based on one criteria	2A			
3.2.2	Sort worksheet data based on multiple criteria	2A			
3.2.3	Insert arithmetic formulas into worksheet cells	3A			
3.2.4	Identify frequently used worksheet functions	3B			
3.2.5	Insert formulas that include worksheet functions into cells	4C			
3.2.6	Modify formulas and functions	3C			
3.2.7	Use AutoSum	3A			

IC³ Module 2 (Key Applications) Objectives		Excel 2002: Level 1 (084200)	Excel 2002: Level 2 (084201)	Word 2002: Level 1 (084300)	Word 2002: Level 2 (084301)
3.2.8	Identify common sources of errors in formulas and functions		4F		
3.2.9	Draw logical conclusions based on worksheet data		5C		
3.2.10	Absolute vs. relative cell addresses	3C, 3D			
3.3	Be able to format a worksheet				
3.3.1	Change number formats	4A			
3.3.2	Specify cell borders and shading	4E			
3.3.3	Specify cell alignment (wrapping, rotation, etc.)	4H			
3.3.4	Create and apply styles	4D			
3.3.5	Apply table AutoFormats	4J			
3.3.6	Use the Format Painter	1D			
3.3.7	Insert a page break	7F			
3.3.8	Create headers and footers	7D			
3.3.9	Set a print area	7G			
3.3.10	Specify scaling for printing	7E			
3.3.11	Set gridlines to print	7E			
3.3.12	Specify repeating rows and columns	7E			
3.4	Add pictures and charts to a worksheet				
3.4.1	Insert and modify pictures in a worksheet		1C		
3.4.2	Insert and manipulate drawn objects into a worksheet		1C		
3.4.3	Create a chart based on worksheet data	6A			
3.4.4	Change chart type	6D			
3.4.5	Modify chart elements	6B			
3.4.6	Be able to identify if a graph accurately represents worksheet data	6A			

Notes

LESSON LABS

Due to classroom setup constraints, some labs cannot be keyed in sequence immediately following their associated lesson. Your instructor will tell you whether your labs can be practiced immediately following the lesson or whether they require separate setup from the main lesson content. Lesson-level lab setup information is listed in the front of this manual in the course setup section.

LESSON 2 LAB 1

Entering and Editing Worksheet Data

Data Files:

- Practice - Office Supplies

Scenario:

You were recently appointed the secretary on the board of a non-profit organization. To keep track of the organization's office supply inventory, you already created an electronic spreadsheet, Practice Office Supplies. However, there are several edits you need to make to this file, so you open it and make the necessary changes so that your file matches Figure 2-1. You then save the file as My Practice - Office Supplies, and finally close it.

	A	B	C	D	E	F
1			Office Supplies			
2						
3	ID	Item		Quantity	Cost per item	
4						
5		1	Pencils	40	0.15	
6		2	Highlighters	15	1.15	
7		3	File folders	100	0.05	
8		4	Note pads	12	1.25	
9		5	Sticky note pads	30	0.75	
10						

Figure 2-1: *The completed file, My Practice Office Supplies.*

1. **Use the task pane to open Practice - Office Supplies.xls from the My Documents folder.**

2. Using Figure 2-1 as a guide, **change the number of pencils to *40* and the cost of Sticky note pads to *0.75*.**

3. **Move the Office Supplies heading in cell A1 to cell B1.**

4. **Insert a row between rows 3 and 4.**

5. **Insert a column before column A that includes the heading text *ID*.**

6. **Use AutoFill to add a series of numbers in column A.**

7. **Apply bold formatting to the worksheet and column heading text.**

8. **Save the file as *My Practice - Office Supplies.xls*.**

9. **Close the file.**

LESSON 3 LAB 1

Performing Calculations

Data Files:

- Practice - Formulas

Scenario:

The board has asked you to report the total inventory cost at its next meeting. So, you open the filed named Practice - Formulas and create formulas that calculate inventory costs for individual items, as well as a total inventory cost. Use Figure 3-1 to check your cost figures. You then save the file as My Practice - Formulas, and finally close it.

	A	B	C	D	E	F	G	H
1		Office Supplies						
2								
3	ID	Item		Quantity	Cost per item		Total inventory cost	
4								
5	1	Pencils		40	0.15		6	
6	2	Highlighters		15	1.15		17.25	
7	3	File folders		100	0.05		5	
8	4	Note pads		12	1.25		15	
9	5	Sticky note pads		30	0.75		22.5	
10						Total:	65.75	

Figure 3-1: *The completed file, My Practice - Formulas.*

1. **Open Practice - Formulas.xls.**

2. In cell **G5, enter a formula that calculates the total inventory cost for pencils.**

3. To calculate the remaining inventory costs, **copy the formula in cell G5 to the G6:G9 range.**

4. In cell G10, **use a built-in function to calculate the total inventory cost.** Your costs should match those in Figure 3-1.

5. **Save the file as** *My Practice - Formulas.xls.*

6. **Close the file.**

LESSON 4 LAB 1

Formatting

Data Files:

- Practice - Formats

Scenario:

Now that you have all the data and calculations in your worksheet, you want to enhance the looks of it. So you open the Practice - Formats file and apply text and numeric formats, emphasize a cell by adding borders and color, reduce the width of a column, and align the contents of a range. Use Figure 4-1 to make these enhancements to your worksheet. You then save the file as My Practice - Formats, and finally close it.

	A	B	C	D	E	F	G	H
1			**Office Supplies**					
2								
3	ID	Item		Quantity	Cost per item		Total inventory cost	
4								
5	1	Pencils		40	0.15		6.00	
6	2	Highlighters		15	1.15		17.25	
7	3	File folders		100	0.05		5.00	
8	4	Note pads		12	1.25		15.00	
9	5	Sticky note pads		30	0.75		22.50	
10						Total:	$65.75	

Figure 4-1: *The completed file, My Practice - Formats.*

1. **Open Practice - Formats.xls.**

2. **Change the font size and font type of the heading text in cell C1 to Times New Roman and 16 pt.**

3. Change the font size and font type of the heading text for the A3:G3 range to Times New Roman and 12 pt.

4. Change the numeric format of the ranges E5:E9 and G5:G9 to Number with two decimal places.

5. Change the numeric format of G10 to Currency with two decimal places.

6. To emphasize the total figure, **apply a border and a fill color of your choice to cell G10.**

7. Reduce the width of column A to *5.00* pixels.

8. Left-align the contents of the A5:A9 range.

9. Save the file as *My Practice - Formats.xls.*

10. Close the file.

LESSON 5 LAB 1

Working with Multiple Worksheets

Data Files:

- Practice - Travel Report

Scenario:

You've been given a file, Practice - Travel Report, that has multiple worksheets that you will now be responsible for updating. Upon review, you rename Sheet 3 as June, move the April sheet so that it is the first sheet in the book, and then you copy the June sheet to the end of the book and make some edits to prepare to enter the July travel figures. You then save the file as My Practice - Travel Report, and finally close it.

1. **Open Practice - Travel Report.xls.**

2. **Rename Sheet 3 as *June*.**

3. To re-order the sheets, **move the April sheet tab to be before the May sheet tab.**

4. **Make a copy of the June sheet, and place it at the end of the book.**

5. **Rename the new sheet as *July*.**

6. On the July sheet, **delete the B5:D14 range and edit the sheet heading text to read** *July Travel Expenses.*

7. Save the file as *My Practice - Travel Report.xls.*

8. **Close the file.**

LESSON 6 LAB 1

Creating and Modifying Charts

Data Files:

- Practice - Chart

Scenario:

You've been asked to create an embedded chart in the Practice - Chart file that represents the units sold in 2002 by territory. So you open the file, and, by using Figure 6-1 as a guide, you create a pie chart, modify it by resizing and moving the legend information, and then change the chart type to a 3D Pie chart. You then save the file as My Practice - Chart, and finally close it.

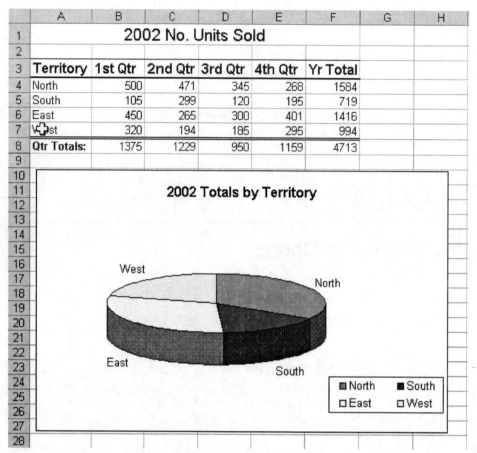

	A	B	C	D	E	F	G	H
1			2002 No. Units Sold					
2								
3	Territory	1st Qtr	2nd Qtr	3rd Qtr	4th Qtr	Yr Total		
4	North	500	471	345	268	1584		
5	South	105	299	120	195	719		
6	East	450	265	300	401	1416		
7	West	320	194	185	295	994		
8	Qtr Totals:	1375	1229	950	1159	4713		

Figure 6-1: *The completed file, My Practice - Chart.*

1.   **Open Practice - Chart.xls.**

2.   Using the Chart Wizard, **create an embedded pie chart that shows the year totals by territory. Include a chart title, category labels, and data labels,** as shown in Figure 6-1.

3.   Using Figure 6-1 as a guide, **resize and move the chart.**

4.   Using Figure 6-1 as a guide, **resize and move the legend information.**

5.   **Change the chart type to a 3D Pie chart.**

6.   **Save the file as** *My Practice - Chart.xls.*

7.   **Close the file.**

LESSON 7 LAB 1

Setting Page Display and Printing Options

Data Files:

• Practice - Sales

Scenario:

You have a worksheet, Practice - Sales, that you need to print. After displaying the file in Print Preview, you decide to set some page display and print options. You insert page breaks so that each division will print on a worksheet, set a print title so that the worksheet title in cell B1 prints on each page, create a custom header that includes the page number and date, and then adjust the margin settings. You then save the file as My Practice - Sales, and finally close it.

1/14/2002   1

Books and Beyond - Sales Report

Eastern USA

Name	1st Qtr	2nd Qtr	3rd Qtr	4th Qtr	Totals
Long	110	175	140	750	1175
Olson	200	210	240	575	1225
Stark	300.9	180	395	1100	1975.9
Todd	150	200.4	125	185	660.4
Unger	220	195	335	1025	1775
TOTAL:	980.9	960.4	1235	3635	6811.3
AVERAGE:	196.18	192.08	247	727	1362.26
HIGH:	300.9	210	395	1100	1975.9

Figure 7-1: *Page 1 of the completed file, My Practice - Sales.*

---

1. **Open Practice - Sales.xls.**

---

2. **Preview the worksheet printout.** The worksheet will print out on one page.

---

3. **Close Print Preview and insert the necessary page breaks so that each of the three divisions will print out on separate pages.**

---

4. **Set a print title for cell B1.**

---

5. From Print Preview, **create a custom header that includes the current data in the left section and the page number in the center section. Delete the default header in the center section.**

---

6.   **Delete the default center footer.**

7.   **Adjust the margins so that the report will print centered on the page horizontally.**

8.   **Close Print Preview and save the file as *My Practice - Sales.xls*.** Your file should look something like Figure 7-1.

9.   **Close the file.**

SOLUTIONS

Lesson 1

Activity 1-1

1. **In the following table, indicate Yes if you would use Excel to accomplish the task or No if you would use another software application to accomplish the task.**

Task	Your Response
You need to create a chart that is linked to a range of data.	*Yes.*
You need to create a list of sales data that includes commission calculations and then sort and filter that data a number of ways.	*Yes.*
You need to create a memo to all department managers.	*No.*
You need to create a database of customers and their addresses.	*No.*
You need to compose a letter to one of your boss's associates.	*No.*
You need to create a monthly budget for your department.	*Yes.*

2. **Which task is best accomplished by using Excel?**

   a) Create a database of your company's client base.

   ✓ b) Calculate sales data for three divisions in your company.

   c) Create a table that includes employee service award intervals and their corresponding gifts.

   d) Create a presentation that includes a table with numerical data.

Activity 1-2

2. In the following graphic, identify the columns, rows, and cells in the worksheet.

Column _C_

Row _A_

Cell _B_

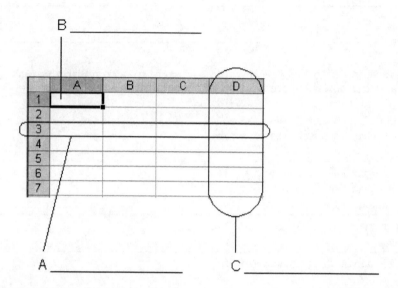

3. Identify the active cell.

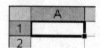

The cell with the bold border is the active cell—cell A1.

4. Identify the text in the cell reference area.

Located above the column A heading, Excel displays the name of the current, or active, cell in the reference area.

5. What is the status of the mode indicator?

In the left corner of the status bar, the mode indicator displays Ready.

Activity 1-5

1. Identify the following elements:

- Standard toolbar.

- Formatting toolbar.
- Move handle on the Standard and Formatting toolbars.
- Buttons on the Standard Docked toolbar.

You can use ScreenTips to identify the buttons on the toolbars.

Use Figure 1-2 and Table 1-1 to help identify the elements.

Activity 1-6

3. **If you want to save the worksheet for the first time, will you use the Save or the Save As command?**

You should use the Save As command the first time you save a file.

Lesson 2

Activity 2-3

3. **Identify the options provided by the Auto Fill Options button.**

You can copy cells, fill the series, fill formatting only, fill without formatting, and fill months.

6. **Identify the options provided by the AutoFill Options button for the Qtr series.**

Notice that the options are different than the previous fill series.

Activity 2-4

3. **What was the effect on the Northeastern Region and Mideastern Region data?**

The inserted row extends across the entire width of the worksheet, splitting the data for these two divisions.

Activity 2-6

2. **What occurred as a result of inserting the blank cells?**

The range M11:P11 shifted to the right to the range N8:Q11.

Activity 2-7

4. **Do you think you can you undo more than one action at once?**

You can use this list to undo several actions at once.

Lesson 3

Activity 3-1

2. What is the sales total of January through April for Employee 123456789?

The value is 562.01.

Activity 3-5

2. Did Excel change the cell addresses relative to their new positions?

Yes.

Activity 3-6

2. What is the result?

As the formula was copied, the references changed relative to their new locations. In this situation, this wasn't the desired outcome. Because the commission rate resides only in cell H3, each commission formula needs to refer to cell H3.

4. What is the result?

The copied formulas refer to cell H3. The dollar signs prevent the cell reference from changing when you copy it.

Lesson 4

Activity 4-1

2. How are the formatted numbers displayed?

Excel displays all numbers in the Number format with two decimal places. Most of the columns have been widened automatically to display the additional formatting characters.

4. What happens when you place the mouse pointer over cell H12?

A ToolTip appears indicating the contents of the cell.

Activity 4-2

2. **What format type will display the numbers like a social security number?**

000-00-0000

Activity 4-4

3. **What elements does the style include?**

The Number option specifies your custom numeric category. The Font option includes the italic attribute you applied above in step 1. The other elements are the default options.

Lesson 7

Activity 7-1

2. **What do you notice about your headings?**

They remain stationary, always displayed at the top of the screen no matter where you are in the file.

NOTES

GLOSSARY

3-D area chart
Used to show a three-dimensional view of an area chart.

3-D bar chart
Used to show a three-dimensional view of a bar chart.

3-D column chart
Used to show a three-dimensional view of a column chart.

3-D line chart
Used to show a three-dimensional view of a line chart. Lines appear as bands.

3-D pie chart
Used to show a three-dimensional view of a pie chart.

absolute reference
A cell reference in a formula that doesn't change when you copy the formula.

active cell
The cell that's selected when Excel creates a new worksheet.

adaptive menus
An Office XP menu that displays menu choices dynamically, based on which choices you use most often.

adaptive toolbars
An Office XP application toolbar that displays buttons dynamically, based on which buttons you use most often.

application window
Usually fills the entire screen and provides an interface for you to interact with Excel.

area chart
Used to graphically display the importance of values over time; emphasizes the amount of change, rather than the time or rate of change.

argument
Data enclosed in parentheses (included in functions).

AutoFormat
A built-in group of cell formats that you can apply to a range of data.

automatic recalculation
Updates the results of formulas containing cell references when you change the contents of the cell to which those formulas refer.

bar chart
Used to graphically display individual values for comparison. Categories are drawn from the vertical axis, and values are drawn from the horizontal axis.

bubble chart
Used to plot and coordinate values. The size of the data marker indicates the value of a third variable. Similar to XY (scatter) charts.

category axis
The horizontal axis on a chart; also known as the x-axis.

cell
The intersection of a column and a row.

cell reference area
Displays the name of the current or active cell.

chart
A graphical representation of worksheet data.

GLOSSARY

chart sheet
A chart that appears on a separate sheet in a workbook.

column
A boundary within a worksheet that extends vertically through all the rows and holds data.

column chart
Used to graphically display individual values for comparison. Categories are drawn from the horizontal axis, and values are drawn from the vertical axis.

cone, cylinder, and pyramid chart
Used to add a dramatic effect to 3-D column and bar charts.

data markers
A chart symbol that represents a single data point.

data points
Worksheet values that appear in a chart.

data series
Column or rows of data from a worksheet that Excel uses to create a chart.

database
An organized collection of information. It differs from a list in the sense that items are collectively grouped using a common theme among each in a database. A list solely displays any number of items, regardless of their relation.

donut chart
Used to graphically display more than one data series. Similar to a pie chart.

embedded chart
A chart that is an object on a worksheet.

fill handle
The box at the corner of a cell or range that you can use to activate the Excel AutoFill feature. When a cell or range of cells contains data that you can display in increments, drag the fill handle to the left, right, up, or down to fill a range with data.

font
The typeface, and size of a set of characters.

footer
Text that prints at the bottom of each page.

formatting
Changes the way that numbers and text appear in a worksheet.

formula
A set of instructions that you enter in a cell to perform calculations.

formula bar
Displays the contents of the active cell in a workbook.

function
A built-in formula.

function argument ToolTip
A link, which displays when you begin typing a formula, that contains a function that you can use to obtain more information about using the specified function.

gridlines
Lines that are drawn in the plot area so that the data markers can easily be compared with an axis value.

header
Text that prints at the top of each page.

legend
The text that identifies the series in a chart.

line chart
Used to graphically show trends over time; emphasizes time flow and rate of change, rather than the amount of change.

mode indicator
Appears on the left side of the status bar and indicates the status of the active cell.

move handle
Used to resize docked toolbars.

order of operations
The sequence that Excel follows when it performs calculations on formulas with more than one operator.

pie chart

Used to graphically display one data series as a whole. Each of its parts represents a percentage of that whole.

radar chart

Used to graphically show changes or frequencies of data relative to a center point and to each other.

range

A rectangular group of adjacent cells in a worksheet.

relative reference

A cell reference in a formula that changes when you copy it relative to its new location on the worksheet.

row

A boundary within a worksheet that extends horizontally through all of the columns and holds data.

series name

The title of the row or column from which the data was taken.

sheet tabs

Used to navigate between worksheets in a workbook.

smart tag

A button that appears when you perform an action or error, such as pasting data, that gives you options related to the action or error.

status bar

Displays information about a selected command and Excel's current state.

stock chart

Used to graphically display the high, low, and close of stock prices.

style

A collection of individual format options that you can apply at the same time to selected cells.

surface chart

Used to show what appears to be a sheet stretched over the category axis. This chart type is useful for finding the optimum combinations between two sets of data. It's similar to a topographic map; color and pattern indicate areas that are in the same range of values (color doesn't mark the data series).

tab scrolling buttons

Used to scroll the display of worksheet tabs one at a time or display the first or last grouping of sheet tabs within a workbook.

task pane

A window which, by default, is displayed on the right side of Excel 2002 that allows you to easily access important commands.

title bar

Located across the top of the application window, the title bar displays the name of the application and the active workbook.

toolbar

Buttons that provide quick access to Excel's most frequently used commands.

value axis

The vertical axis on the chart; also known as the y-axis.

workbook

A file that contains three worksheets by default. These worksheets can be different types, such as worksheets, macro sheets, or chart sheets.

workbook window

Appears within the application window and displays a workbook in which to enter and store data.

worksheet

A single sheet of the workbook containing text, numbers, and formulas.

XY (scatter) chart

Used to plot coordinate values; shows the relationship between numeric values in several data series.

NOTES

INDEX

INDEX

data points, 132

data series, 132, 136

databases, 3

donut charts, 123

E

Edit mode, 7

embedded charts, 125

Enter mode, 7

F

files

  naming, 21, 22

  saving, 21, 22

Fill Color feature, 90, 93

fill handle, 38, 70, 71

Find And Replace feature, 47, 48, 49, 94

fonts, 85

  changing size, 85

  changing typeface, 85

footers, 155

  creating, 156, 157

  inserting, 156, 157

format painter, 17

formatting, 16

formula bar, 5

formulas, 58

  copying, 70, 71

  creating, 58, 59, 73

  editing, 73

  entering, 59, 61, 63

  modifying, 60

  using mathematical symbols, 59

function argument ToolTips, 65

functions, 64

  creating a formula, 65, 66, 69

G

Go To command, 102

gridlines, 132, 136

H

headers, 155

  creating, 156, 157

  inserting, 156, 157

Help, 25

  choosing a method, 24

  obtaining, 25

L

Landscape page orientation, 159

legends, 132, 136

line charts, 123

M

margins, 152

  modifying, 154

  setting, 153, 154

Merge And Center button, 101, 102

mode indicator, 7

move handles, 17

moving data, 30, 31

N

Narrow Column ToolTip, 80

navigating techniques

  using the keyboard, 12

  using the mouse, 12

New Workbook task pane, 30, 31

non-adjacent cells, 70

non-adjacent ranges, 16

number formats

  applying a custom format, 83

  creating a custom format, 82, 83

  identifying, 78

  using the Format Cells dialog box, 79, 80

O

Office Assistant, 25

order of operations, 58

P

page breaks, 161

  adding, 161, 162

  modifying, 161

  removing, 161, 162

page orientations, 159

  changing, 159, 160

Paste Options feature, 34, 35

pie charts, 123

plot area, 136

Portrait page orientation, 159

print ranges

  printing, 164

  setting, 164

  specifying, 163

print titles

  defining, 150

  setting, 150, 151

NOTES